YOUR
MINIATURE
PINSCHER

By Buris R. Boshell, M. D.

Second Printing

Compiled and Edited by
William W. Denlinger and R. Annabel Rathman

DENLINGER'S

P.O. Box 76
Fairfax, Virginia 22030

I dedicate this book to Martha, for love, patience, and devotion, who without reluctance for her unrewarded efforts, graciously leads a "dogs life"; and to Patty and Tom-Tom, whose willingness to share me and my avocation makes it all worthwhile.

Buris R. Boshell, M. D.

International Standard Book Number 0-87714-024-3
Library of Congress Catalogue Card Number: 69-19733

The Author, Dr. Buris R. Boshell, and Ch. Bo-Mar's Johnny Come Lately.

Foreword

As a farm boy, I had the opportunity, in collaboration with a few cousins, to collect and to "tame" more or less successfully a retinue of quail, crows, rabbits, fox, raccoons, squirrels, flying squirrels, and birds of all varieties. This early interest in animals led to a B. S. degree in Agriculture, graduate school in animal breeding, and Veterinary School at Auburn University between 1943-1949. During this time I established a small herd of purebred Jersey cattle and a small kennel of Irish Setters and Cocker Spaniels on the family farm. These replaced my all-time favorite, "Rover," a combination of Shepherd, Collie, and miscellany, who dogged my steps from the day I walked until the day he died.

My decision to make the veterinary side of life an avocation and human medicine my vocation, led to a trek to New England for eight years at Harvard and necessitated the dispersal of my cattle and kennel, but not my desire to continue an interest in animal breeding. The spark was renewed by a gift of a Boxer puppy from a patient when I was a senior assistant resident physician at Peter Bent Brigham Hospital in Boston. A visit to Grayarlin Kennels and a talk with the owners, George Pusey and Jane Kamp, led to an introduction to the world of dog shows at a Sanction Match in Lowell, Massachusetts, where we garnered our first ribbon—a First in the Puppy Class under Ken Tiffin. A few more shows convinced us that we had a pet but not a show Boxer.

We were bitten, so we purchased a top one, Van's Blythe Spirit, who put us on "cloud nine" by winning Second in the Open Class at the American Boxer Club and First in Open at Westminster shortly after we purchased her. She later became our first champion, first Group winner, and the dam of more Group-winning champions, as well as the double granddam of our Grand Futurity winner. Subsequently, we purchased from Rebel Roc a Min-Pin puppy, Rebel Roc's Cora von Kurt, who proved that she was for us in Min-Pins what Blythe was in Boxers—a top show dog, a warm companion, and a wonderful producer—thus establishing our kennel and our motto, "GOOD PUPPIES HAVE GOOD MOTHERS."

Buris R. Boshell, M. D.

1969

Contents

Ch. Rebel Roc's Casanova v. Kurt when he won his seventy-fifth all-breed Best in Show at Perkiomen Valley, Penna., in August 1963. Breeder, Mrs. E. W. Tipton, Jr. Handler, Mr. E. W. Tipton, Jr.

Selecting a Miniature Pinscher Puppy

There are those who claim they can select the future show dog at a few hours or a few days of age. I do not have this ability and thus cannot comment adequately as to how it is done. One can, however, do a certain amount of "culling" soon after delivery. Congenital anomalies such as cleft palates, hare lips, dew claws, etc., should be looked for when the puppy is cleaned up after parturition. Furthermore, disqualifying marks, such as large white spots (which must be less than one half inch in greatest diameter when the animal is grown) and thumb prints, can be recognized when the animal is quite young. It is, however, important to realize that small white spots and a few black hairs in the rust markings of the forelegs, present at birth, may disappear as the animal matures.

Not until the puppies are old enough to demonstrate a little personality and individuality (i.e., about five to seven weeks of age) do I feel secure in starting to grade the pups and make selections. One should look for a puppy that is happy and outgoing without a trace of shyness. The puppy should already appear reasonably balanced at this age—i.e., head in proportion to body, etc. The tail should be up, and the pup should be curious about his surroundings and eager to explore. At this age the muzzle should be reasonably strong and broad. The eyes should be almost, but not quite, round, and they should be well set in their sockets. Already, slight chiselling under the eyes should be apparent. The jaws should not be markedly undershot or overshot. However, it is not possible at this age to be definitely sure whether the mouth is going to be good or bad. The ears should be set high, and a suggestive flatness should be apparent in the forehead. A few wrinkles which may be present on the head at this time may well disappear. However, if excessive wrinkling is evident, a good head rarely develops. If the muzzle is already thin and refined at this age, the eventual result will almost invariably be a "snipey" muzzle, frequently accompanied by "pop eyes" and an "apple head," all of which are undesirable. Such undesirable characteristics are more likely to be found in very small rather than in medium sized or larger pups.

The neck should be long and the body short. Thus, if one is attempting to select the best puppy in a litter, merely picking out the puppy with the shortest back and the longest neck is a reasonable start. The topline should be level, and the chest should already be down to the elbows. Later on—between three and six months of age—the puppy will likely go through a stage when the chest does not reach the elbows, and this balance may not be re-achieved until the puppy is a year of age or, occasionally, older. At six weeks of age, however, the balance should be correct. The chest cage should be full and the loin short. The feet should be in proportion to the other aspects of the puppy. Unusually large feet frequently presuppose excessive size and coarseness.

One should look for disqualifying points, such as white spots and thumb prints, and for cryptorchidism in a male regardless of the age. Although there is considerable difference in opinion on this subject, in my experience one can usually find the testicles in the male pup by four to six weeks of age. Fortunately, the problem of cryptorchidism does not appear to be a common one in the Miniature Pinscher breed.

Although one prefers to find good straight front legs, even at six weeks of age, these features are not always present even when they are going to be so at a later date. This is especially true in the smaller pup, who, in my experience, is a slower maturer in this breed than are the larger puppies. I have frequently erred in ruling a pup out at five to six weeks of age because the front legs were not quite as straight as I desired, only to find out later that a rather dramatic improvement had appeared. On the other hand, if the stifle is too straight at this age, I have never seen it appear any way other than straighter as the puppy matures. The pup that appears unusually well-angulated or perhaps over-angulated at this age may have some difficulty in maintaining a good stance of the rear end or even in moving properly without "hocking, either in or out" at this point, and yet later on have a perfectly acceptable rear end assembly. Slowly but surely I am coming around to the conviction that a Min-Pin that is just a hair straighter in stifle than our breed Standard calls for

8

may actually move better in the rear than one with an unusually long stifle—who is frequently over-angulated also. I am not advocating straight stifles, however, because the animal with the straight stifle cannot drive in the rear with the authority that the properly angulated dog can.

Although it is possible at an early age to detect faults in movement, such as loose shoulders, throwing the elbows out, and crossing over in front or rear, one cannot be certain about movement until the puppy is four months or more of age. I have seen good movement get worse, but rarely have I seen a poor movement get better. Thus, if a six-week-old puppy is throwing an elbow out, one will frequently find the statement, "He'll get better when he matures and tightens up," is only wishful thinking.

Color of the pup will change considerably after he is six weeks of age. The coat of the solid red and the rust markings of the black and rust will usually darken considerably. The darker the red coloring at this point, however, the darker it will be in proportion when the dog matures.

If one is looking only for a pet, perhaps it is all right to select the pup at six weeks of age. In this case, temperament should be uppermost in mind. Thus, the safest thing to do is to select the friendliest, healthiest puppy in the litter. If a show quality animal is desired, however, the prospective buyer should evaluate the puppy at this age along the preceding guidelines but delay making his final selection until the pup is four to six months of age, at which time the ears should have been trimmed and should be standing properly, and the movement can be more easily evaluated.

To evaluate movement one should observe the animal moving directly away and look especially for elbows that are being thrown out or rear legs that are crossing. Subsequently, when the animal has been turned and is moving toward the prospective buyer, it is easy to note front movement that is too close or too wide and also whether or not the rear legs are moving at a proper distance apart.

A side view when the animal is moving should reveal soft backs, high rear ends, etc., that are not infrequently seen in the Min-Pin.

Perhaps all of this should have been prefaced by stating that one of the most important aspects of puppy selection is the selection of

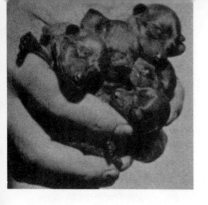

"A handful" of puppies from Half-Tot, owned by Mr. and Mrs. Henry Stephens, Carletonville, South Africa. Total weight of the five puppies was 10½ ounces.

a reputable breeder who will advise one honestly and intelligently. Names and addresses of Min-Pin breeders who have puppies available are included in the advertising sections of the dog publications on sale at local pet shops or available on the reference shelves of most public libraries. Lists of breeders may also be secured by writing the Miniature Pinscher Club of America or one of the Regional Miniature Pinscher Clubs listed in the various dog publications. Also, a prospective purchaser may write The American Kennel Club, Inc., 51 Madison Avenue, New York, N. Y. 10010, and request a list of Miniature Pinscher breeders in his area.

If one has in mind the possibility of using the purchase to establish a breeding program, then it is important that the puppy not only be of good conformation and temperament but also be the product of a good dam and sire and preferably line bred. It is much more important that the puppy be out of a bitch and by a sire that are proven producers of quality than it is to just select a youngster who happens to be sired by the current big winner. One should be quite wary of buying from a kennel that makes a practice of selling all of its show quality bitches and keeping the culls for brood stock, or from

Lenhenri's Nancy (dam of Half-Tot) with seven of her eight puppies. Owners, Mr. and Mrs. Henry Stephens, Carletonville, South Africa.

the breeder who keeps oversized bitches for production because they have larger litters and are easier whelpers.

The general tendency of a new owner is to pick up the puppy and hold it in his lap on the trip from the kennel to the new home. This is reasonably satisfactory if one is careful to prevent the puppy from jumping out of his hands and getting hurt, and if the new owner is willing to chance the possible "accident" in his lap or, more likely, encounter a seizure of vomiting on the way home. Miniature Pinschers usually develop into excellent travelers. However, it is not at all unusual for the new puppy, because of nervousness, excitement, etc., to become nauseated and perhaps vomit during his initial automobile ride. Therefore, it is better for all concerned, including the puppy, to bring a nice clean crate to transport the puppy back home. The bottom of the crate should be lined with clean newspapers, some of which may be torn into shreds to allow the puppy to build a nest. Furthermore, a puppy is more likely to be happy on the ride if a safe chew stick, which most pet stores have available, is placed in the crate to entertain the youngster on the excursion home.

Generally, by the time the puppy has ridden a few miles, he will be settled down and quite happy in his crate. In fact, the crate will probably represent a security symbol and perhaps a tie-in with his old home, even after he has been unloaded into new surroundings.

It is preferable to arrange to pick up the new puppy prior to feeding time and to feed him soon after his arrival in his new home so that he will associate the change with a degree of pleasure. Furthermore, if it is possible for the new owner to spend all of his time with the youngster for the first day or two, it will likely be found to be advantageous for both the puppy and the new owner, for they will then have an opportunity to learn what to expect from each other. The attention supplied by the new owner gives the puppy a feeling of security. And an opportunity to romp with his new master soon convinces him that the new home has brought on new challenges and new kinds of fun—which frequently make up entirely for the things he left back in the kennel. As a matter of fact, Miniature Pinscher puppies thrive on attention, and many develop a great deal more personality when separated from the other puppies in the litter and given more human association.

Ch. Sanbrook Showoff, shown here winning W. D. from the Puppy Class at the Trenton Specialty under Dr. B. R. Boshell. Handler, Phyllis King Wolf.

Generally speaking, it is wise for the new owner to take his puppy to the veterinarian at the earliest possible time. Furthermore, it is a safeguard for the kennel owner who has sold the new puppy to have a veterinarian examine the puppy in detail and be in a position to assure the new owner that the puppy is in first-class condition at the time he moves into the new home. Since the pup will be frightened, however, it is wise to suggest to the veterinarian that the puppy be handled carefully. The veterinarian should record the previous health record of the puppy, including his shots, etc., and check the puppy for evidence of infection, or any physical abnormality. It is also wise for the veterinarian to check for intestinal parasites and to make definitive plans for providing the additional shots, etc., that are needed by the puppy.

If plans are being made to show the puppy at a later date, it is wise for the veterinarian to use a different type of table from the kind used for dog shows. It is really just a matter of encouraging pleasant associations with everything related to shows. Since it is not possible to make all aspects of nail trimming, shots, and other

Ch. Halrok's Happy Talk, shown here taking a Five Point Major at the Eugene Kennel Club Show under Mrs. B. Godsol, September 1967. Owners, Dave and Sherrie Krogh (K-Roc Kennels).

veterinary procedures pleasant to the puppy, it is important to dis-associate all veterinary procedures from the show training and the actual showing of the puppy. The Miniature Pinscher must learn to stand quietly on the table for the judge's examination, and he is much more likely to do so happily if he has no memories of unpleasant experiences on a similar table.

The puppy should be registered as soon as possible after he is obtained by the new owner. A pedigree, along with the individual registration application, should be obtained from the seller. The registration form should be filled in completely by the seller and should include the date of sale, the name and address of the new owner, the date of transfer, etc. If the puppy is to be named by the seller, the name should be filled in completely at the time the puppy is transferred. If the naming is to be left up to the new owner, then the subject should be discussed in some detail with the seller so that if the new owner desires to include the kennel name of the seller, written permission is obtained on the application blank at this time. Frequently, the old as well as the new owner will wish to collaborate on the name.

Both first and second choice names should be listed on the front of the application, and the total number of letters in the name should not exceed twenty-three. The registration procedure is rather long at best. Therefore, it is important to make sure that no mistakes are made. Specifically, one should be doubly careful to make sure that he has included the check or money order to cover the registration fee because The American Kennel Club will not start the processing of registration requests which are not accompanied by the registration fee. The registration process has to take place each time the puppy is transferred. Therefore, if the puppy is being bought from a dealer or individual who has previously purchased the puppy from the breeder, it is important to make sure that the original transfer has been recorded properly.

Show training may begin at any age and should continue for the entire show life of the animal. One should make out a definite plan for training, in much the same manner that he would lay out an educational program for a child. A part of the plan should be at least a mental if not a verbal description of what the end product should be. So let's analyze what constitutes a good show dog and then design a program that should help achieve the goal.

13

Ch. Bel Roc's Dobe v. Enztal, one of the all-time great sires, bred and owned by Mr. and Mrs. Booher.

Ch. Sergeant Fritz v. Enztal, owned by Mr. and Mrs. F. P. Booher.

Bel-Roc's Snicklefritz v. Enztal, bred and owned by Mrs. Maisie Booher.

Ch. Adrian of Flomo, bred by Lila Niederluecke and owned by Lila Niederluecke and Mark Reel.

First of all, basic breed conformation must be apparent. Contrary to the views of many "ringside quarterbacks," a real "bum" can rarely be shown or promoted into a big winner. Thus, if we start out with a pup who has the potential to become a champion, then we have the basic merchandise to sell in the ring, but it must be "packaged" properly.

The pup must learn to move on a leash. He must learn to stand on a table for inspection. And he must do these things with enough animation and enthusiasm to be appealing to the judge and, hopefully, to the ringside as well. One might put himself in the dog's position and ask, "Just why should I move on a leash, and why should I stand on a table for people to look at me and some stranger run his hands over my body, open my mouth, and criticize me silently if not verbally?" Then it isn't too difficult to surmise that going through these maneuvers doesn't just come naturally to the dog. So how are they developed? It is my opinion that good performance is "bought" from the dog by rewards that may either be a word or pat of approval from his handler, or something more substantial, such as a morsel of liver, cheese, or other tidbit. In any case, the show ring should be a place of fun, expectation, and enjoyment for both the dog and the handler, and the show training should develop these attitudes.

An approach that may prove quite successful is to bring one or two pups into an enclosed area, along with a dish of raw hamburger or other appealing delicacy, and then reward the fledgling with a taste of the tidbit each time he wanders over to you. If the puppy declines to approach you initially, he may be stimulated to do so by bringing a seasoned show dog into the training area and allowing the puppy to compete with the veteran for the food that is offered. Generally speaking, it is easier to get training underway when at least two animals are loose in the training area—so long as the animals involved do not engage in combat or in too much frivolity.

After the pup is following his handler around the training area, looking him in the eye, pleading for a handout, and ignoring most of the distractions that are available, the second phase of training may begin. That is the conditioning of the pup to the lead or collar around the neck. A soft slip lead may be eased over the pup's head and placed loosely around the neck. At this stage of the

Ch. Merry Hill's Voodoo Wing.

Ch. Sunburst of Alema.

Ch. Merry Hill's Miss Spitfire.

Ch. Greywing Hi Steppin Gigolo.

training, don't be too surprised if the animal complains to "high heaven" and simulates an angry mustang with a burr under the saddle. This reaction is always temporary, and in my opinion presupposes a degree of intelligence, fire, and spirit, which will later stand the dog in good stead in the show ring.

The puppy should be allowed to drag the leash around behind him for a while until he becomes used to it and proceeds to ignore it when tidbits are offered. At this point the handler may take hold of the lead and slowly condition the puppy to the fact that the lead may limit the radius of his movement slightly. At all times, however, the pup must be assured that it is fun to be near the handler and that frequent rewards—kind words, soft pats, and tidbits—will be offered.

The handler may now walk away from the pup, holding the lead until it becomes slightly taut, then offer a treat until the puppy is enticed to advance to him. He then repeats the procedure until finally the pup is following without too much urging and is moving the entire length or circumference of the training area on the leash. A good puppy, properly handled, can usually be leash trained in five or ten training sessions of fifteen minutes each, conducted once or twice daily.

If the training program is to be successful, it is imperative that you heed the following cautionary advice: Do not attempt to train a puppy when you are rushed or emotionally upset. And do not at any time speak harshly, or drag, jerk, or strike the puppy during a training session.

An interesting shot of Coster Flight, 1966 Junior Champion of the World, showing the true Hackney gait.

The Adult
Miniature Pinscher

The Miniature Pinscher is a smooth coated dog in the Toy Group. He is frequently incorrectly referred to as a Miniature Doberman. The characteristics that distinguish the Miniature Pinscher are his size (ten to twelve and a half inches), his racy elegance, and the Hackney gait which he exhibits in a self-possessed, animated, cocky manner. Now to consider the specific features of the breed, as set forth in the Miniature Pinscher Standard.

Head: The head should by no means be a replica of the Doberman Pinscher head. From the view in front the head should resemble a blunt wedge, with good chiselling under the eyes, in contrast to the filled-in area in the Doberman. The skull should appear reasonably flat and should taper toward the muzzle. The muzzle should be strong and clean but not coarse. The cheeks should be flat. The lips should be clean and tight.

The ears should be high and reasonably closely set. They should be carried erect and the tips should be well pointed when cropped. The eyes should be slightly oval and set wide apart but fitted cleanly into the orbital sockets. Although the eyes are widely set, when the head is viewed from in front the lateral canthus of the eye (that is, the angle formed by the junction of the upper and lower lids) should be well within the lateral margins of the head. The expression should be one of animation, but not of agitation. The eyes should be dark, shiny, and bright. The rims of the eyelids and the epicanthal folds (the folds at the inner corners of the eyelids) should be well pigmented. The nose should be black except in the chocolates, which may have a self-colored nose. The planes of the skull and the muzzle should be parallel to each other and separated by only a barely perceptible stop, about midway between the occiput and the tip of the nose. The under jaw should be well developed. The teeth should be in good alignment and should meet in a scissors bite.

Common faults in the head are skulliness, lack of chiselling under the eyes, pop eyes, pig eyes, light colored eyes, too much roundness of the skull (i. e., apple head), light colored noses, and undershot

Ch. Houck's Jigger of Blu-Stone winning First in Group, Southern Adirondack Kennel Club, August 10, 1963. Handled by breeder-owner Arnold E. Houck.

mouths or poorly developed under jaws that give an "Andy Gump" appearance.

Neck: The neck should be clean, long, and slightly arched, blending into shoulders that are well laid back. There should be no dewlap or loose wrinkling of the neck.

Common faults are short, bully necks, flabbiness or excessive folds of skin on the anterior surface of the neck. Another common fault is the appearance of a roll on the dorsal surface of the body at the point where the neck joins the body. This is sometimes due to excessive weight on the animal.

Body: The body of the Miniature Pinscher should be wedge shaped, tapering toward the rear. The ribs should be well sprung but not too barrelled. The brisket should drop to the elbows when viewed from the side and should be clearly apparent. The back should be level or perhaps slope slightly toward the rear. The body should be square—i. e., the height at the withers should equal the length, although it is perfectly acceptable for females to be slightly longer.

Ch. Eldomar Court Jester. Never beaten by a male Min-Pin, Jester was B. O. S. to Ch. Patzie v. Mill-Mass every time he was shown, with the exception of the Beverly-Riviera Show, where he is shown winning the breed under Mrs. Murray Brooks.

When viewed from the rear, the tail should be straight and set high, and the spring of the rib should be apparent beyond the outline of the rear quarters.

When the animal is viewed from in front, the brisket should be clean and rounded. The barrel of the chest should be smooth and apparent but not coarse or knobby. The shoulders (i. e., the scapulae) should be well laid back and should be about the same length as the humerus (i. e., the upper bone of the forelegs). These bones should meet at approximately a ninety degree angle.

Legs: The front pasterns should be almost straight but flexible. A very slight bend of the pastern is acceptable. The feet should be tight, well padded, and compact, but in all respects adequate to support the weight of the animal. The stifle should be relatively long and gently curving. The hocks should be well let down and should be perpendicular to a line drawn from the floor. The hocks should turn neither in nor out, either when the dog is moving or standing still.

Movement: The animal should move with a true Hackney gait— i. e., front legs lifted smartly and high with a bend at the "wrist" and all movement within the outline of the body, yet not close in front, and there should be no tendency of the front legs to cross over. Failure to exhibit the true Hackney gait should be severely penalized since this is one of the distinguishing features of the breed.

From the rear the animal should move out with real spring and drive. Again, the rear legs should move within the outlines of the body, but not close unless the animal is moving rapidly—in which case it is proper for the feet to move in toward the center of gravity. Unfortunately, this fact does not appear to be well understood and frequently a dog that is only doing what comes normally and naturally is improperly penalized.

Faults in movement: Throwing the elbows, crossing over in front, moving too closely or occasionally too widely in rear, and, worst of all, failure to present a typical Hackney gait.

Coat: The coat should be short, relatively fine, and tight fitting. It should be clean and shiny. Coat color may be red, stag red, black and rust, chocolate and rust, or blue and rust. The rich dark clear red or the lustrous black with rich dark rust markings is preferred.

Ch. Heming's Tiny Tiger of Hei-Dan winning Best in Show at Parkersburg, W. Va., at eleven months from Bred-by-Exhibitor Class.

The appearance of a white spot larger than one-half inch in its widest diameter or the appearance of thumb marks constitutes a disqualification. Heights of less than ten inches and more than twelve and a half inches are also disqualifying factors.

Common body faults: Low tailset, high rear end, sway back, shilliness (i. e., lack of spring of rib and shallow chest), excessive length of the body, and lumpiness or knobbiness of the body.

The Miniature Pinscher should be well balanced and typey. The term "typey" refers to the definitive characteristics that separate the Miniature Pinscher from other breeds as defined in the breed Standard. Also, the ideal Miniature Pinscher should be animated, alert, vigorous, and interested in his surroundings. He should look and act like the "King of the Toys."

Before discussing the particular attributes of conformation that distinguish the Miniature Pinscher of excellence, I would like first

Ch. Crown Prinz von Siegenburg, with owner-handler Capt. A. C. Berry and judge William Pym.

22

of all to call attention to an important aspect of the Miniature Pinscher as a show dog. That aspect is temperament—for good temperament is of the utmost importance. Regardless of conformation, the shy Miniature Pinscher is never going to make his mark in the show ring. It is important to concentrate on producing Miniature Pinschers of outgoing, friendly personality who keep their tail up in the show ring and demonstrate a fearless outlook toward all that approaches them.

The Min-Pin should be amenable to handling by strangers without showing signs of fear or anger. In the kennel, however, it is perfectly acceptable for the Miniature Pinscher to be basically selective and somewhat reserved. But he should not be shy or vicious. The Miniature Pinscher who pulls himself together and moves out with a "devil may care" attitude cannot keep from catching the eye of the judge. In this regard it is of interest that many times the judge viewing the Toy Group fails to remember that the smooth coated animal such as the Miniature Pinscher cannot hide a single fault in the manner that the long coats in the Group do. And I fear that frequently the Miniature Pinscher is unduly penalized for small blemishes that are obvious, when careful inspection would indicate faults of much greater magnitude in the long coated members of the Group.

Starting at the head (since this is the portion that is to be seen first by the judge in the ring) one looks for a nice strong muzzle of proper proportion on a well chiseled head. The head should, of course, be in proportion to the neck and body. The eyes should be dark and oval in shape. They should be neither the pop eye of the Chihuahua or Pekingese nor the small almond shaped eye of the Doberman. The ears should be closely set and erect and trimmed so that they appear to grow right out of the head and blend into the head outline. It is more important that not too much bell or burr be left on the ear, thereby giving a bat or butterfly appearance. The neck should be long, clean, and well arched and should join the head onto a sound, smooth body. Manchester heads and Chihuahua heads are equally undesirable in the Miniature Pinscher. The very small Miniature Pinscher frequently has the latter type head and the very large Min-Pin oftentimes has the former type. Although one hears the statement that it is easy to develop heads in a breeding program, I think that this is wishful thinking and that

23

Ch. Midnight Jewel v. Haymount, bitch.

Ch. Midnight Sun v. Haymount, male.

Ch. Midnight Magic v. Haymount, bitch.

These three Miniature Pinschers represent an all-champion litter. Bred and owned by W. A. Van Story, Jr., the three were handled by Mr. James J. Geddes.

we must make every effort to have the proper type head on all of our animals.

The topline should be smooth and straight. It is acceptable for the topline to slope slightly to the rear but very unbecoming when it slopes in the opposite manner—which, unfortunately, is not uncommon. The tail should be high and carried in a jaunty manner. A low tail set destroys the sharp, clean outline that a good Miniature Pinscher exhibits. Also, a high rear end and a soft back always detract considerably from the outline that we are looking for. Unfortunately, a poor topline can be missed if an animal is not moved properly so the judge can get a good look at the silhouette. It is rather disconcerting to have selected the winner and then to have him moved across where a good side view is provided and note an extreme dip in the back. An astute handler, by appearing not to understand the instructions of the judge, can make it difficult for the judge to see this defect, for instead of making a clear side view possible, he may move the dog in a very short circle and only at an angle to the judge, rather than providing a parallel sweep across the ring whereby the judge can really see the outline of the dog well.

The body should be relatively short, giving the animal a square appearance, but it should not be so short and cobby that it interferes with proper movement. I have seen Miniature Pinschers that were so short that they "crabbed" in moving—which is certainly not desirable. Furthermore, an unusually short body is all too often accompanied by the short, bully neck that gives the Miniature Pinscher a knobby appearance when he is viewed in silhouette. The rib cage should be well sprung and the brisket should be easily apparent. The dog should not be overdone from this standpoint, however, nor should he be shallow, shelly, or slabsided.

The really good Miniature Pinscher that is going to win well through the years will frequently not have the brisket and rib spring that is desired, until he is about a year and a half or two years of age. The puppy that is completely mature in appearance at six to eight months of age is quite unlikely to hold this beautiful "show girl" figure into the ripe old adulthood of six or seven years of age. As a matter of fact, it is quite striking to note the slow and very pleasing maturity that occurs in puppies that are strongly bred

25

Urray Golden Penny II, C.D.X., Can. C.D., at Spokane Kennel Club, receiving trophy for High Scoring Dog, with score of 199 in Open B.

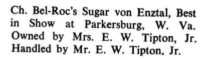

Ch. Bel-Roc's Sugar von Enztal, Best in Show at Parkersburg, W. Va. Owned by Mrs. E. W. Tipton, Jr. Handled by Mr. E. W. Tipton, Jr.

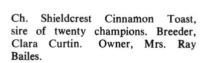

Ch. Haldee von Glick, owned by Tom and Avis Flynn.

Ch. Shieldcrest Cinnamon Toast, sire of twenty champions. Breeder, Clara Curtin. Owner, Mrs. Ray Bailes.

from the Dobe v. Enztal bloodline. The racy, elegant puppy usually attains maturity of chest and brisket late. This type does have to be watched closely for size, however.

Attempts to hold size down by withholding adequate nutrition is a mistake. As a matter of fact, this more frequently results in malformed bodies than in an overall decrease in height. By the same token, it is important not to let the puppies get so extremely fat as to cause undue stress and strain on legs which are not developed enough to carry the weight. This rarely presents a problem, however, because usually the puppy (unlike so many humans) will eat just enough to stay in top condition, if challenged with food of good quality on a regular basis.

The rear legs should be strong, well muscled and angulated, with hocks that are well let down. There is no reason why one should not develop rear ends on Miniature Pinschers comparable to those seen in the good moving working dogs such as the Doberman Pinscher. Certainly it is imperative to insist that if we are going to use the term "King of the Toys" for the Miniature Pinscher, then he should be sounder, and a better mover, than members of most of the other Toy breeds.

Genetics certainly enters into the development of the rear end just as it does other aspects of the body. By the same token, controlled exercise is essential in order to realize the full potential that genetics has provided the youngster. The breeder who has provided hills and dales in his paddocks is certainly in an extremely advantageous position as compared with the person who has nothing but flat concrete runs or small cages in which to develop his youngsters. Fortunately, hip dysplasia is rare in the Miniature Pinscher breed. However, in some of the smaller animals it is not too uncommon to see a variant of Legg Perthes disease, or slipped patellae. Chances are that improper handling and injuries sustained during puppyhood, plus inadequate exercise, account for poor rear ends as often as does genetics.

It is very interesting to note that a dog that has a rather straight stifle sometimes gets by under the judge much more successfully than does the one who is a little bit more angulated, with a long stifle. The straight stifled animal cannot move too closely in the rear, generally speaking, nor is he likely to hock in or out. Furthermore, especially in the young puppy that is extremely well angulated or

27

Ch. Sanbrook Sentry v. Spritelee. Breeder, Ann Dutton. Owners, Mr. and Mrs. Wm. Lee.

Ch. Mudhen Acre's Happy Heart. Owner-handler, Hank Hearn.

Ch. Dazan's Mister Bear winning the Group at Contra Costa Kennel Club.

Best in Show Winner Ch. Peniwil's Nuttin But Trash.

perhaps even overly so, it is some time before the ability to handle his rear end is developed properly. And I suspect that if the proper exercise is not provided, together with good nutrition and good care, many of these dogs never do develop the kind of movement that we are looking for.

When the dog moves away, the rear feet should be in line with the body and not moving in or out. By the same token, it is important to remember that as the dog moves faster, he tends to move his feet in towards the center of gravity. Thus, it is not proper to penalize a dog for merely doing what comes naturally. He should not "knit," nor should he move too widely in the rear, however. The barrel shaped rear is not as objectionable as the close, narrow rear, but it still constitutes a fault.

The Miniature Pinscher is supposed to have a Hackney gait, and a proper front is essential for proper gait. A Hackney gait is not a lot of extraneous movement of the front legs but a very specific movement. It is not merely raising a stiffly held leg high—and, all too frequently, wide and handsome. Instead, the front legs should be lifted straight forward and moderately high but with a slight bend of the ankle—in other words, not as a straight arm. I will accept a slight (though not extreme) looseness of the shoulder and close movement in front in preference to the straight, stiff leg movement or pacing.

The Hackney movement is clearly demonstrated in the picture facing the first page of this chapter. In order that the Miniature Pinscher may move properly, the front legs must be straight and youthful. All four legs must be sound and adequate to support the animal, but not coarse and heavy. The feet should be tight and well padded. While I don't feel that the term "cat's paw" is really quite applicable to the feet of any Miniature Pinschers I have seen, it is important to avoid the hare foot which creeps into the breed very easily.

The coat should be short, smooth, hard, and relatively fine, in keeping with the size of the dog. Coat color is important because it adds a great deal of beauty when it is of proper shade and hue. Many individuals state that color really is not important and that conformation is everything. This certainly is not true, although I will accept the view that color is less important than sound con-

29

Ch. Bo-Mar's Drum Son of Jay-Mac.

Axel v. d. Trouwe Vriendjes.

Ch. Chrijstel v. d. Trouwe Vriendjes.

"Kleo," bred by Mrs. A. Rätz.

Swedish and Danish Ch. Arko.

Swedish Ch. Kicki, bred by Mrs. A. Rätz.

formation. By the same token, one cannot keep from being impressed by the deep, clear, dark red dog or the black and rust with extremely rich rust markings. The stag red or the very light red is not as desirable. In the black and rust, the rust markings should appear above each eye, on the muzzle, cheeks, throat, chest, forelegs (lower half), vent, and inside the hind legs as well as on the lower portion of the hocks and feet. Pencil striped black markings should appear on the toes. The black may be replaced by blue or chocolate, although these colors are relatively rare.

The Standard for the Miniature Pinscher requires that the size be between ten and twelve and a half inches. This is a reasonably large spread and I am not advocating that it be changed. But I think it is quite important that breeders try to narrow the spread to something like eleven to twelve inches. Certainly the *dog* that is between eleven and twelve inches frequently will be sounder in conformation and will stand out more readily in the Toy Group than will the unusually tiny specimen. Frequently, if the dog is larger than twelve and a half inches, a degree of coarseness is evident, the head structure is not really typical, and many of the fine features of the Miniature Pinscher are lost.

Following is the "Scale of Points" appended to the official Miniature Pinscher Standard approved by The American Kennel Club. While the judging of dogs cannot be reduced to a strictly mathematical procedure, the "Scale of Points" is of the utmost significance for it indicates the relative importance of the various aspects of the dog.

SCALE OF POINTS

General appearance & movement		Body	15
(very important)	30	Feet	5
Skull	5	Legs	5
Muzzle	5	Color	5
Mouth	5	Coat	5
Eyes	5	Tail	5
Ears	5		
Neck	5	TOTAL	100

31

Ch. Hans von Tejas, U. D.

Ch. Merrie Angel of Merry Hills, B. I. S. Winner.

Ch. Helms' Gunner General, Group Winner.

Ch. Haasmor Dineh Babe, B. I. S. Winner.

Grooming the Family Dog

Every dog should be taught from puppyhood that a grooming session is a time for business, not for play. He should be handled gently, though, for it is essential to avoid hurting him in any way. Grooming time should be pleasant for both dog and master.

A light, airy, pleasant place in which to work is desirable, and it is of the utmost importance that neither dog nor master be distracted by other dogs, cats, or people. Consequently, it is usually preferable that grooming be done indoors.

Before each session, the dog should be permitted to relieve himself. Once grooming is begun, it is important to avoid keeping the dog standing so long that he becomes tired. If a good deal of grooming is needed, it should be done in two or more short periods.

A sturdy grooming table is desirable. The dog should stand on the grooming table while the back and upper portions of his body are groomed, and lie on his side while underparts of his body are brushed, nails clipped, etc.

It is almost impossible to brush too much, and show dogs are often brushed for a full half hour a day, year round. If you cannot brush your dog every day, you should brush him a minimum of two or three times a week. Brushing removes loose skin particles and stimulates circulation, thereby improving condition of the skin. It also stimulates secretion of the natural skin oils that make the coat look healthy and beautiful.

Before brushing, any burs adhering to the coat, as well as matted hair, should be carefully removed, using the fingers and coarse toothed comb with a gentle, teasing motion to avoid tearing the coat. The coat should first be brushed lightly in the direction in which the hair grows. Next, it should be brushed in the opposite direction, a small portion at a time, making sure the bristles penetrate the hair to the skin, until the entire coat has been brushed thoroughly and all loose soil removed. Then the coat should be brushed in the direction the hair grows, until every hair is sleekly in place.

The dog that is kept well brushed needs bathing only rarely. Once or twice a year is usually enough. If it is necessary to bathe a puppy, extreme care must be exercised so that he will not become chilled. No dog should be bathed during cold weather and then permitted to go outside immediately. Whatever the weather, the dog should always be given a good run outdoors and permitted to relieve himself before he is bathed.

Various types of "dry baths" are available, and in general, they are quite satisfactory when circumstances are such that a bath in water is impractical. Dry shampoos are usually worked into the dog's coat thoroughly, then removed by towelling or brushing.

Before starting a water bath, the necessary equipment should be assembled. This includes a tub of appropriate size, preferably one that has a drain so that the water will not accumulate and the dog will not be kept standing in water throughout the bath. A rubber mat should be placed in the bottom of the tub to prevent the dog from slipping. A small hose with a spray nozzle—one that may be attached to the water faucet—is ideal for wetting and rinsing the coat, but if such equipment is not available, then a second tub or a large pail should be provided for bath and rinse water. A metal or plastic cup for dipping water, special dog shampoo, a small bottle of mineral or olive oil, and a supply of absorbent cotton should be placed nearby, as well as a supply of heavy towels, a wash cloth, and the dog's combs and brushes. Bath water and rinse water should be slightly warmer than lukewarm, but should not be hot.

To avoid accidentally getting water in the dog's ears, place a small amount of absorbent cotton in each. With the dog standing in the tub, wet his body by using the hose and spray nozzle or by using the cup to pour water over him. Take care to avoid wetting the head, and be careful to avoid getting water or shampoo in the eyes. (If you should accidentally do so, placing a few drops of mineral or olive oil in the inner corner of the eye will bring relief.) When the dog is thoroughly wet, put a small amount of shampoo on his back and work the lather into the coat with a gentle, squeezing action. Wash the entire body and then use the cup and container of water (or hose and spray nozzle) to rinse the dog thoroughly.

Dip the wash cloth into clean water, wring it out enough so it won't drip, then wash the dog's head, taking care to avoid the eyes. Remove the cotton from the dog's ears and sponge them gently, inside and out. Shampoo should never be used inside the ears, so if they are extremely soiled, sponge them clean with cotton saturated with mineral or olive oil. (Between baths, the ears should be cleaned frequently in the same way.)

Quickly wrap a towel around the dog, remove him from the tub, and towel him as dry as possible. To avoid getting an impromptu bath yourself, you must act quickly, for once he is out of the tub, the dog will instinctively shake himself.

While the hair is still slightly damp, use a clean comb or brush to remove any tangles. If the hair is allowed to dry first, it may be completely impossible to remove them.

So far as routine grooming is concerned, the dog's eyes require little attention. Some dogs have a slight accumulation of mucus in the corner of the eyes upon waking mornings. A salt solution (a teaspoon of table salt to one pint of warm, sterile water) can be sponged around the eyes to remove the stain. During grooming sessions it is well to inspect the eyes, since many breeds are prone to eye injury. Eye problems of a minor nature may be treated at home (see page 54), but it is imperative that any serious eye abnormality be called to the attention of the veterinarian immediately.

Feeding hard dog biscuits and hard bones helps to keep tooth surfaces clean. Slight discoloration may be readily removed by rubbing with a damp cloth dipped in salt or baking soda. The dog's head should be held firmly, the lips pulled apart gently, and the teeth rubbed lightly with the dampened cloth. Regular care usually keeps the teeth in good condition, but if tartar accumulates, it should be removed by a veterinarian.

If the dog doesn't keep his nails worn down through regular exercise on hard surfaces, they must be trimmed at intervals, for nails that are too long may cause the foot to spread and thus spoil the dog's gait. Neglected nails may even grow so long that they will grow into a circle and puncture the dog's skin. Nails can be cut easily with any of the various types of nail trimmers. The cut is made just outside the faintly pink bloodline that can be seen on white nails. In pigmented nails, the bloodline is not easily seen, so the cut should be made just outside the hooklike projection on the underside of the nails. A few downward strokes with a nail file will smooth the cut surface, and, once shortened, nails can be kept short by filing at regular intervals.

Care must be taken that nails are not cut too short, since blood vessels may be accidentally severed. Should you accidentally cut a nail so short that it bleeds, apply a mild antiseptic and keep the dog quiet until bleeding stops. Usually, only a few drops of blood will be lost. But once a dog's nails have been cut painfully short, he will usually object when his feet are handled.

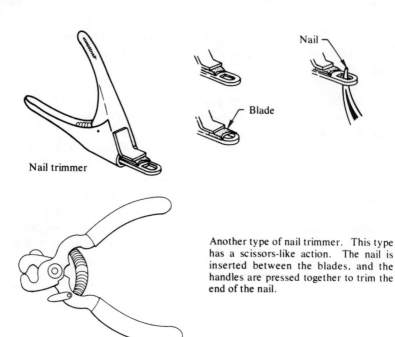

Nail

Blade

Nail trimmer

Another type of nail trimmer. This type has a scissors-like action. The nail is inserted between the blades, and the handles are pressed together to trim the end of the nail.

Dog crate with grooming-table top provides rigid, well supported surface on which to groom dog, and serves as indoor kennel for puppy or grown dog. Rubber matting provides non-slip surface. Dog's collar may be attached to adjustable arm.

Centered below is a grooming table with an adjustable arm to which the dog's collar may be attached. The adjustable arm at right below may be clamped to an ordinary table or other rigid surface which will serve as a grooming table.

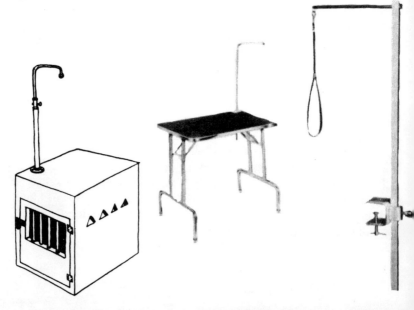

"Bed and Board" for the Family Dog

It is much easier to adapt to the demands of a new puppy if you collect the necessary equipment before you bring him home. You will need a water and food dish—preferably stainless steel and of a type that will not tip easily. You will need some chew toys, a soft puppy lead, and a soft hair brush for puppy grooming. You will need to decide where your dog is going to sleep and to prepare his bed.

Every dog should have a bed of his own, snug and warm, where he can retire undisturbed when he wishes to nap. And, especially with a small puppy, it is desirable to have the bed arranged so the dog can be securely confined at times, safe and contented. If the puppy is taught early in life to stay. quietly in his box at night, or when the family is out, the habit will carry over into adulthood and will benefit both dog and master.

The dog should never be banished to a damp, cold basement, but should be quartered in an out-of-the-way corner close to the center of family activity. His bed can be an elaborate cushioned affair with electric warming pad, or simply a rectangular wooden box or heavy paper carton, cushioned with a clean cotton rug or towel. Actually, the latter is ideal for a new puppy, for it is snug, easy to clean, and expendable. A "door" can be cut on one side of the box for easy access, but it should be placed in such a way that the dog can still be confined when desirable.

The shipping crates used by professional handlers at dog shows make ideal indoor quarters. They are lightweight but strong, provide adequate air circulation, yet are snug and warm and easily cleaned. . For the dog owner who takes his dog along when he travels, a dog crate is ideal, for the dog will willingly stay in his accustomed bed during long automobile trips, and the crate can be taken inside motels or hotels at night, making the dog a far more acceptable guest.

Dog crates are made of chromed metal or wood, and some have tops covered with a special rubber matting so they can be used as grooming tables. Anyone moderately handy with tools can construct a crate similar to the one illustrated on the opposite page.

Crates come in various sizes, to suit various breeds of dogs. For reasons of economy, the size selected for a puppy should be adequate for use when the dog is full grown. If the area seems too large when the puppy is small, a temporary cardboard partition can be installed to limit the area he occupies.

For the owner's convenience and to enhance the dog's sense of security, food and water dishes may be kept in the same general area where the crate is kept.

Nutrition

The main food elements required by dogs are proteins, fats, and carbohydrates. Vitamins A, B complex, D, and E are essential, as are ample amounts of calcium and iron. Nine other minerals are required in small amounts but are amply provided in almost any diet, so there is no need to be concerned about them.

The most important nutrient is protein and it must be provided every day of the dog's life, for it is essential for normal daily growth and replacement of body tissues burned up in daily activity. Preferred animal protein products are beef, mutton, horse meat, and boned fish. Visceral organs—heart, liver, and tripe—are good but if used in too large quantities may cause diarrhea (bones in large amounts have the same effect). Some veterinarians feel that pork is undesirable, while others consider lean pork acceptable as long as it is well cooked. Bacon drippings are often recommended for inclusion in the dog's diet, but this is a matter best discussed with your veterinarian since the salt in the bacon drippings might prove harmful to a dog that is not in good health. The "meat meal" used in some commercial foods is made from scrap meat processed at high temperatures and then dried. It is not quite so nutritious as fresh meat, but in combination with other protein products, it is an acceptable ingredient in the dog's diet.

Cooked eggs and raw egg yolk are good sources of protein, but raw egg white should never be fed since it may cause diarrhea. Cottage cheese and milk (fresh, dried, and canned) are high in protein, also. Puppies thrive on milk and it is usually included in the diet until the puppy is about three months of age, but when fed to older dogs it often causes diarrhea. Soy-bean meal, wheat germ meal, and dried brewers yeast are vegetable products high in protein and may be used to advantage in the dog's diet.

Vegetable and animal fats in moderate amounts should be used, especially if a main ingredient of the diet is dry or kibbled food. Fats should not be used excessively or the dog may become overweight. Generally, fats should be increased slightly in the winter and reduced somewhat during warm weather.

Carbohydrates are required for proper assimilation of fats. Dog biscuits, kibble, dog meal, and other dehydrated foods are good sources of carbohydrates, as are cereal products derived from rice, corn, wheat, and ground or rolled oats.

Vegetables supply additional proteins, vitamins, and minerals, and by providing bulk are of value in overcoming constipation. Raw or cooked carrots, celery, lettuce, beets, asparagus, tomatoes, and cooked spinach may be used. They should always be chopped or ground well and mixed with the other food. Various combinations may be used, but a good home-mixed ration for the mature dog consists of two parts of meat and one each of vegetables and dog meal (or cereal product).

Dicalcium phosphate and cod-liver oil are added to puppy diets to ensure inclusion of adequate amounts of calcium and Vitamins A and D. Indiscriminate use of dietary supplements is not only unjustified but may be harmful and many breeders feel that their over-use may lead to excessive growth as well as to overweight at maturity. Also, kidney damage in adult dogs has been traced to over-supplementation of the diet with calcium and Vitamin D.

Foods manufactured by well-known and reputable food processors are nutritionally sound and are offered in sufficient variety of flavors, textures, and consistencies that most dogs will find them tempting and satisfying. Canned foods are usually "ready to eat," while dehydrated foods in the form of kibble, meal, or biscuits may require the addition of water or milk. Dried foods containing fat sometimes become rancid, so to avoid an unpalatable change in flavor, the manufacturer may not include fat in dried food but recommend its addition at the time the water or milk is added.

Candy and other sweets are taboo, for the dog has no nutritional need for them and if he is permitted to eat them, he will usually eat less of foods he requires. Also taboo are fried foods, highly seasoned foods, and extremely starchy foods, for the dog's digestive tract is not equipped to handle them.

Frozen foods should be thawed completely and warmed at least to lukewarm, while hot foods should be cooled to lukewarm. Food should be in a fairly firm state, for sloppy food is difficult for the dog to digest.

Whether meat is raw or cooked makes little difference, so long as the dog is also given the juice that seeps from the meat during cooking. Bones provide little nourishment, although gnawing bones helps make the teeth strong and helps to keep tartar from accumulating on them. Beef bones, especially large knuckle bones, are best. Fish, poultry, and chop bones should never be given to dogs since they have a tendency to splinter and may puncture the dog's digestive tract.

Clean, fresh, cool water is essential and an adequate supply should be available twenty-four hours a day from the time the puppy is big enough to walk. Especially during hot weather, the drinking pan should be emptied and refilled at frequent intervals.

Puppies usually are weaned by the time they are six weeks old, so when you acquire a new puppy ten to twelve weeks old, he will already have been started on a feeding schedule. The breeder should supply exact details as to number of meals per day, types and amounts of food offered, etc. It is essential to adhere to this established routine, for drastic changes in diet may produce intestinal upsets. In most instances, a combination of dry meal, canned meat, and the plastic wrapped hamburger-like products provide a well-balanced diet. For a puppy that is too fat or too thin, or for one that has health problems, a veterinarian may recommend a specially formulated diet, but ordinarily, the commercially prepared foods can be used.

The amount of food offered at each meal must gradually be increased and by five months the puppy will require about twice what he needed at three months. However, the puppy should not be allowed to become too fat. Obesity has become a major health problem for dogs, and it is estimated that forty-one percent of American dogs are overweight. It is essential that weight be controlled throughout the dog's lifetime and that the dog be kept in trim condition—neither too fat nor too thin—for many physical problems can be traced directly to overweight. If the habit of overeating is developed in puppyhood, controlling the weight of the mature dog will be much more difficult.

A mature dog usually eats slightly less than he did as a growing puppy. For mature dogs, one large meal a day is usually sufficient, although some owners prefer to give two meals. As long as the dog enjoys optimum health and is neither too fat nor too thin, the number of meals a day makes little difference.

The amount of food required for mature dogs will vary. With canned dog food or home-prepared foods (that is, the combination of meat, vegetables, and meal), the approximate amount required is one-half ounce of food per pound of body weight. If the dog is fed a dehydrated commercial food, approximately one ounce of food is needed for each pound of body weight. Most manufacturers of commercial foods provide information on packages as to approximate daily needs of various breeds.

For most dogs, the amount of food provided should be increased slightly during the winter months and reduced somewhat during hot weather when the dog is less active.

As a dog becomes older and less active, he may become too fat. Or his appetite may decrease so he becomes too thin. It is necessary to adjust the diet in either case, for the dog will live longer and enjoy better health if he is maintained in trim condition. The simplest way to decrease or increase body weight is by decreasing or increasing the amount of fat in the diet. Protein content should be maintained at a high level throughout the dog's life.

If the older dog becomes reluctant to eat, it may be necessary to coax him with special food he normally relishes. Warming the food will increase its aroma and usually will help to entice the dog to eat. If he still refuses, rubbing some of the food on the dog's lips and gums may stimulate interest. It may be helpful also to offer food in smaller amounts and increase the number of meals per day. Foods that are highly nutritious and easily digested are especially desirable for older dogs. Small amounts of cooked, ground liver, cottage cheese, or mashed, hard-cooked eggs should be included in the diet often.

Before a bitch is bred, her owner should make sure that she is in optimum condition—slightly on the lean side rather than fat. The bitch in whelp is given much the same diet she was fed prior to breeding, with slight increases in amounts of meat, liver, and dairy products. Beginning about six weeks after breeding, she should be fed two meals per day rather than one, and the total daily intake increased. (Some bitches in whelp require as much as 50% more food than they consume normally.) She must not be permitted to become fat, for whelping problems are more likely to occur in overweight dogs. Cod-liver oil and dicalcium phosphate should be provided until after the puppies are weaned.

The dog used only occasionally for breeding will not require a special diet, but he should be well fed and maintained in optimum condition. A dog used frequently may require a slightly increased amount of food. But his basic diet will require no change so long as his general health is good and his flesh is firm and hard.

Dishes of this type are available in both plastic and stainless steel.

Crockery dish for food or water.

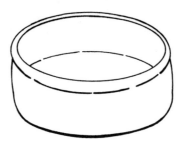

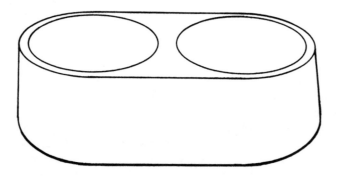

Stainless steel dish for food and water.

Maintaining the Dog's Health

In dealing with health problems, simple measures of preventive care are always preferable to cures—which may be complicated and costly. Many of the problems which afflict dogs can be avoided quite easily by instituting good dog-keeping practices in connection with feeding and housing.

Proper nutrition is essential in maintaining the dog's resistance to infectious diseases, in reducing susceptibility to organic diseases, and, of course, in preventing dietary deficiency diseases.

Cleanliness is essential in preventing the growth of disease-producing bacteria and other micro-organisms. All equipment, especially water and food dishes, must be kept immaculately clean. Cleanliness is also essential in controlling external parasites, which thrive in unsanitary surroundings.

Symptoms of Illness

Symptoms of illness may be so obvious there is no question that the dog is ill, or so subtle that the owner isn't sure whether there is a change from normal or not. **Loss of appetite, malaise** (general lack of interest in what is going on), **and vomiting** may be ignored if they occur singly and persist only for a day. However, in combination with other evidence of illness, such symptoms may be significant and the dog should be watched closely. **Abnormal bowel movements,** especially diarrhea or bloody stools, are causes for immediate concern. **Urinary abnormalities** may indicate infections, and bloody urine is always an indication of a serious condition. When a dog that has long been housebroken suddenly becomes incontinent, a veterinarian should be consulted, for he may be able to suggest treatment or medication that will be helpful.

Fever is a positive indication of illness and consistent deviation from the normal temperature range of 100 to 102 degrees is cause for concern. Have the dog in a standing position when taking his temperature. Coat the bulb of a rectal thermometer with petroleum jelly, raise the dog's tail, insert the thermometer to approximately half its length, and hold it in position for two minutes. Clean the thermometer with rubbing alcohol after each use and be sure to shake it down.

Fits, often considered a symptom of worms, may result from a variety of causes, including vitamin deficiencies, or playing to the point of exhaustion. A veterinarian should be consulted when a fit occurs, for it may be a symptom of serious illness.

Persistent coughing is often considered a symptom of worms, but may also indicate heart trouble—especially in older dogs.

Stary coat—dull and lackluster—indicates generally poor health and possible worm infestation. **Dull eyes** may result from similar conditions. Certain forms of blindness may also cause the eyes to lose the sparkle of vibrant good health.

Vomiting is another symptom often attributed to worm infestation. Dogs suffering from indigestion sometimes eat grass, apparently to induce vomiting and relieve discomfort.

Accidents and Injuries

Injuries of a serious nature—deep cuts, broken bones, severe burns, etc.—always require veterinary care. However, the dog may need first aid before being moved to a veterinary hospital.

A dog injured in any way should be approached cautiously, for reactions of a dog in pain are unpredictable and he may bite even a beloved master. A muzzle should always be applied before any attempt is made to move the dog or treat him in any way. The muzzle can be improvised from a strip of cloth, bandage, or even heavy cord, looped firmly around the dog's jaws and tied under the lower jaw. The ends should then be extended back of the neck and tied again so the loop around the jaws will stay in place.

A stretcher for moving a heavy dog can be improvised from a rug or board, and preferably two people should be available to transport it. A small dog can be carried by one person simply by grasping the loose skin at the nape of the neck with one hand and placing the other hand under the dog's hips.

Burns from chemicals should first be treated by flushing the coat with plain water, taking care to protect the dog's eyes and ears. A baking soda solution can then be applied to neutralize the chemical further. If the burned area is small, a bland ointment should be applied. If the burned area is large, more extensive treatment will be required, as well as veterinary care.

Burns from hot liquid or hot metals should be treated by applying a bland ointment, provided the burned area is small. Burns over large areas should be treated by a veterinarian.

Electric shock usually results because an owner negligently leaves an electric cord exposed where the dog can chew on it. If possible, disconnect the cord before touching the dog. Otherwise, yank the cord from the dog's mouth so you will not receive a shock when you try to help him. If the dog is unconscious, artificial respiration and stimulants will be required, so a veterinarian should be consulted at once.

Fractures require immediate professional attention. A broken bone should be immobilized while the dog is transported to the veterinarian but no attempt should be made to splint it.

Poisoning is more often accidental than deliberate, but whichever the case, symptoms and treatment are the same. If the poisoning is not discovered immediately, the dog may be found unconscious. His mouth will be slimy, he will tremble, have difficulty breathing, and possibly go into convulsions. Veterinary treatment must be secured immediately.

If you find the dog eating something you know to be poisonous, induce vomiting immediately by repeatedly forcing the dog to swallow a mixture of equal parts of hydrogen peroxide and water. Delay of even a few minutes may result in death. When the contents of the stomach have been emptied, force the dog to swallow raw egg white, which will slow absorption of the poison. Then call the veterinarian. Provide him with information as to the type of poison, and follow his advice as to further treatment.

Some chemicals are toxic even though not swallowed, so before using a product, make sure it can be used safely around pets.

Severe bleeding from a leg can be controlled by applying a tourniquet between the wound and the body, but the tourniquet must be loosened at ten-minute intervals. Severe bleeding from head or body can be controlled by placing a cloth or gauze pad over the wound, then applying firm pressure with the hand.

To treat minor cuts, first trim the hair from around the wound, then wash the area with warm soapy water and apply a mild antiseptic such as tincture of metaphen.

Shock is usually the aftermath of severe injury and requires immediate veterinary attention. The dog appears dazed, lips and tongue are pale, and breathing is shallow. The dog should be wrapped in blankets and kept warm, and if possible, kept lying down with his head lower than his body.

Bacterial and Viral Diseases

Distemper takes many and varied forms, so it is sometimes difficult for even experienced veterinarians to diagnose. It is the number one killer of dogs, and although it is not unknown in older dogs, its victims are usually puppies. While some dogs do recover, permanent damage to the brain or nervous system is often sustained. Symptoms may include lethargy, diarrhea, vomiting, reduced appetite, cough, nasal discharge, inflammation of the eyes, and a rise in temperature. If distemper is suspected, a veterinarian must be consulted at once, for early treatment is essential. Effective preventive measures lie in inoculation. Shots for temporary immunity should be given all puppies within a few weeks after whelping, and the permanent inoculations should be given as soon thereafter as possible.

Hardpad has been fairly prevalent in Great Britain for a number of years, and its incidence in the United States is increasing. Symptoms are similar to those of distemper, but as the disease progresses, the pads of the feet harden and eventually peel. Chances of recovery are not favorable unless prompt veterinary care is secured.

Infectious hepatitis in dogs affects the liver, as does the human form, but apparently is not transmissible to man. Symptoms are similar to those of distemper, and the disease rapidly reaches the acute state. Since hepatitis is often fatal, prompt veterinary treatment is essential. Effective vaccines are available and should be provided all puppies. A combination distemper-hepatitis vaccine is sometimes used.

Leptospirosis is caused by a micro-organism often transmitted by contact with rats, or by ingestion of food contaminated by rats. The disease can be transmitted to man, so anyone caring for an afflicted dog must take steps to avoid infection. Symptoms include vomiting, loss of appetite, diarrhea, fever, depression and lethargy, redness of eyes and gums, and sometimes jaundice. Since permanent kidney damage may result, veterinary treatment should be secured immediately.

Rabies is a disease that is always fatal—and it is transmissible to man. It is caused by a virus that attacks the nervous system and is present in the saliva of an infected animal. When an infected animal bites another, the virus is transmitted to the new victim. It may also enter the body through cuts and scratches that come in contact with saliva containing the virus.

All warm-blooded animals are subject to rabies and it may be transmitted by foxes, skunks, squirrels, horses, and cattle as well as dogs. Anyone bitten by a dog (or other animal) should see his physician immediately, and health and law enforcement officials should be notified. Also, if your dog is bitten by another animal, consult your veterinarian immediately.

In most areas, rabies shots are required by law. Even if not required, all dogs should be given anti-rabies vaccine, for it is an effective preventive measure.

Dietary Deficiency Diseases

Rickets afflicts puppies not provided sufficient calcium and Vitamin D. Symptoms include lameness, arching of neck and back, and a tendency of the legs to bow. Treatment consists of providing adequate amounts of dicalcium phosphate and Vitamin D and exposing the dog to sunlight. If detected and treated before reaching an advanced stage, bone damage may be lessened somewhat, although it cannot be corrected completely.

Osteomalacia, similar to rickets, may occur in adult dogs. Treatment is the same as for rickets, but here, too, prevention is preferable to cure. Permanent deformities resulting from rickets or osteomalacia will not be inherited, so once victims recover, they can be used for breeding.

External Parasites

Fleas, lice, mites, and ticks can be eradicated in the dog's quarters by regular use of one of the insecticide sprays with a four to six weeks' residual effect. Bedding, blankets, and pillows should be laundered frequently and treated with an insecticide. Treatment for external parasites varies, depending upon the parasite involved, but a number of good dips and powders are available.

Fleas may be eliminated by dusting the coat thoroughly with flea powder at frequent intervals during the summer months when fleas are a problem.

Flea collars are very effective in keeping a dog free of fleas. However, some animals are allergic to the chemicals in the collars, so caution must be observed when the collar is used and the skin of the neck area must be checked frequently and the collar removed if the skin becomes irritated. Care must also be taken that the collar is not fastened too tightly, and any excess at the end must be cut off to prevent the dog from chewing it. The collar should be removed if it becomes wet (or even damp) and should always be removed before the dog is bathed and not replaced around the dog's neck again until the coat is completely dry. For a dog which reacts to the flea collar, a medallion to be hung from the regular collar is available. This will eliminate direct skin contact and thus any allergic reaction will be avoided. The medallion should, of course, be removed when the dog is bathed.

Lice may be eradicated by applying dips formulated especially for this purpose to the dog's coat. A fine-toothed comb should

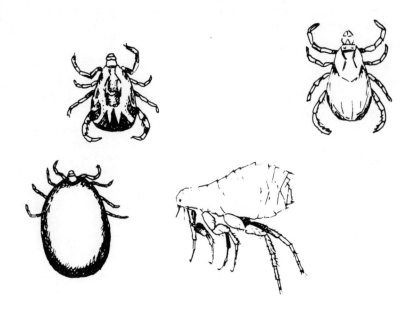

Common external parasites. Above, American dog ticks—left, female and right, male (much enlarged). Lower left, female tick, engorged. Lower right, dog flea (much enlarged).

then be used to remove dead lice and eggs, which are firmly attached to the coat.

Mites live deep in the ear canal, producing irritation to the lining of the ear and causing a brownish-black, dry type discharge. Plain mineral oil or ear ointment should be swabbed on the inner surface of the ear twice a week until mites are eliminated.

Ticks may carry Rocky Mountain spotted fever, so, to avoid possible infection, they should be removed from the dog only with tweezers and should be destroyed by burning (or by dropping them into insecticide). Heavy infestation can be controlled by sponging the coat daily with a solution containing a special tick dip.

Among other preparations available for controlling parasites on the dog's body are some that can be given internally. Since dosage must be carefully controlled, these preparations should not be used without consulting a veterinarian.

Internal Parasites

Internal parasites, with the exception of the tapeworm, may be transmitted from a mother dog to the puppies. Infestation may also result from contact with infected bedding or through access to a yard where an infected dog relieves himself. The types that may infest dogs are roundworms, whipworms, tapeworms, hookworms, and heartworms. All cause similar symptoms: a generally unthrifty appearance, stary coat, dull eyes, weakness and emaciation despite a ravenous appetite, coughing, vomiting, diarrhea, and sometimes bloody stools. Not all symptoms are present in every case, of course.

A heavy infestation with any type of worm is a serious matter and treatment must be started early and continued until the dog is free of the parasite or the dog's health will suffer seriously. Death may even result.

Promiscuous dosing for worms is dangerous and different types of worms require different treatment. So if you suspect your dog has worms, ask your veterinarian to make a microscopic examination of the feces, and to prescribe appropriate treatment if evidence of worm infestation is found.

LIFE CYCLE OF THE HEARTWORM

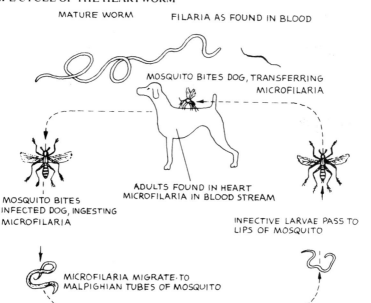

MATURE WORM   FILARIA AS FOUND IN BLOOD

MOSQUITO BITES DOG, TRANSFERRING MICROFILARIA

ADULTS FOUND IN HEART
MICROFILARIA IN BLOOD STREAM

MOSQUITO BITES INFECTED DOG, INGESTING MICROFILARIA

INFECTIVE LARVAE PASS TO LIPS OF MOSQUITO

MICROFILARIA MIGRATE TO MALPIGHIAN TUBES OF MOSQUITO

— — — DEVELOPMENT IN ONE MONTH - - - -

Heartworms were once thought to be a problem confined to the Southern part of the United States but they have become an increasingly common problem in Middle Western States. The larva is transmitted from dog to dog through the bite of the mosquito, and eight to nine months may elapse from the time the dog is bitten until the heartworm is mature. Once they have entered the bloodstream, heartworms mature in the heart, where they interfere with heart action. Symptoms include lethargy, chronic coughing, and loss of weight. Having the dog's blood examined microscopically is the only way the tiny larvae (called microfilaria) can be detected. Eradication of heartworms is extremely difficult, so a veterinarian well versed in this field should be consulted. In an area where mosquitoes are prevalent, it is well to protect the dog by keeping him in a screened-in area.

Hookworms are found in puppies as well as adult dogs. When excreted in the feces, the mature worm looks like a thread and is about three-quarters of an inch in length. Eradication is a serious problem in areas where the soil is infested with the worms, for the dog may then become reinfested after treatment. Consequently, medication usually must be repeated at intervals, and the premises—including the grounds where the dog exercises—must be treated and must be kept well drained. You may wish to consult your veterinarian regarding the vaccine for the prevention of hookworms in dogs which was licensed recently by the United States Department of Agriculture.

Roundworms are the most common of all the worms that may infest the dog, for most puppies are born with them or become infested with them shortly after birth. Roundworms vary in length from two to eight inches and can be detected readily through microscopic examination of the feces. At maturity, upon excretion, the roundworm will spiral into a circle, but after it dies it resembles a cut rubber band.

If you suspect that a puppy may have roundworms, check its gums and tongue. If the puppy is heavily infested, the worms will cause anemia and the gums and the tongue will be a very pale pink color. If the puppy is anemic, the veterinarian probably will prescribe a tonic in addition to the proper worm medicine.

Tapeworms require an intermediate host, usually the flea or the louse, but they sometimes are found in raw fish, so a dog can become infested by swallowing a flea or a louse, or by eating infested fish.

LIFE CYCLE OF THE HOOKWORM

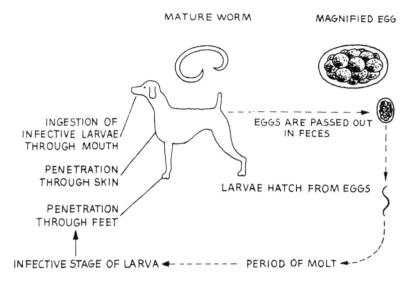

MATURE WORM

MAGNIFIED EGG

INGESTION OF INFECTIVE LARVAE THROUGH MOUTH

EGGS ARE PASSED OUT IN FECES

PENETRATION THROUGH SKIN

LARVAE HATCH FROM EGGS

PENETRATION THROUGH FEET

INFECTIVE STAGE OF LARVA ← ─ ─ ─ ─ ─ PERIOD OF MOLT ←─ ─

LIFE CYCLE OF THE COMMON ROUNDWORM

MATURE WORM

EGG MAGNIFIED 400 TIMES

DOG INGESTS EMBRYONATED EGGS
SHELL DIGESTED OFF WORM IN DOGS STOMACH

EMBRYONATES IN 7 DAYS
IN WARM WEATHER

LARVA PENETRATES THROUGH INTESTINE INTO BLOOD. CIRCULATES FOR SEVERAL DAYS.

IS CAUGHT IN LUNGS, PENETRATES THROUGH TO AIR SIDE OF LUNGS.

EMBRYO GROWS TO MATURITY, LAYS EGGS WHICH ARE PASSED OUT IN FECES.

DOG COUGHS UP EMBRYO, SWALLOWS IT

LIFE CYCLE OF THE FLEA-HOST TAPEWORM

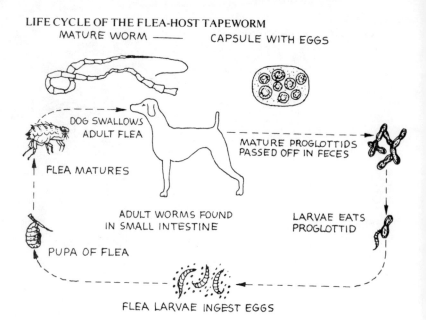

MATURE WORM ——— CAPSULE WITH EGGS

DOG SWALLOWS ADULT FLEA

MATURE PROGLOTTIDS PASSED OFF IN FECES

FLEA MATURES

ADULT WORMS FOUND IN SMALL INTESTINE

LARVAE EATS PROGLOTTID

PUPA OF FLEA

FLEA LARVAE INGEST EGGS

A complete tapeworm can be two to three feet long. The head and neck of the tapeworm are small and threadlike, while the body is made up of segments like links of a sausage, which are about half an inch long and flat. Segments of the body separate from the worm and will be found in the feces or will hang from the coat around the anus and when dry will resemble dark grains of rice.

The head of the tapeworm is imbedded in the lining of the intestine where the worm feeds on the blood of the dog. The difficulty

LIFE CYCLE OF THE WHIPWORM

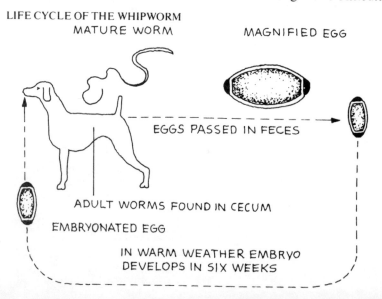

MATURE WORM   MAGNIFIED EGG

EGGS PASSED IN FECES

ADULT WORMS FOUND IN CECUM

EMBRYONATED EGG

IN WARM WEATHER EMBRYO DEVELOPS IN SIX WEEKS

in eradicating the tapeworm lies in the fact that most medicines have a laxative action which is too severe and which pulls the body from the head so the body is eliminated with the feces, but the implanted head remains to start growing a new body. An effective medication is a tablet which does not dissolve until it reaches the intestine where it anesthetizes the worm to loosen the head before expulsion.

Whipworms are more common in the eastern states than in states along the West Coast, but whipworms may infest dogs in any section of the United States. Whipworms vary in length from two to four inches and are tapered in shape so they resemble a buggy whip—which accounts for the name.

At maturity the whipworm migrates into the caecum, where it is difficult to reach with medication. A fecal examination will show whether whipworms are present, so after treatment, it is best to have several examinations made in order to be sure the dog is free of them.

Skin Problems

Skin problems usually cause persistent itching. However, **follicular mange** does not usually do so but is evidenced by moth-eaten-looking patches, especially about the head and along the back. **Sarcoptic mange** produces severe itching and is evidenced by patchy, crusty areas on body, legs, and abdomen. Any evidence suggesting either should be called to the attention of a veterinarian. Both require extensive treatment and both may be contracted by humans.

Allergies are not readily distinguished from other skin troubles except through laboratory tests. However, dog owners should be alert to the fact that various coat dressings and shampoos, or simply bathing the dog too often, may produce allergic skin reactions.

Eczema is characterized by extreme itching, redness of the skin and exudation of serous matter. It may result from a variety of causes, and the exact cause in a particular case may be difficult to determine. Relief may be secured by dusting the dog twice a week with a soothing powder containing a fungicide and an insecticide.

Other Health Problems

Clogged anal glands cause intense discomfort, which the dog may attempt to relieve by scooting himself along the floor on his haunches. These glands, located on either side of the anus, se-

crete a substance that enables the dog to expel the contents of the rectum. If they become clogged, they may give the dog an unpleasant odor and when neglected, serious infection may result. Contents of the glands can be easily expelled into a wad of cotton, which should be held under the tail with the left hand. Then, using the right hand, pressure should be exerted with the thumb on one side of the anus, the forefinger on the other. The normal secretion is brownish in color, with an unpleasant odor. The presence of blood or pus indicates infection and should be called to the attention of a veterinarian.

Eye problems of a minor nature—redness or occasional discharge—may be treated with a few drops of boric acid solution (2%) or salt solution (1 teaspoonful table salt to 1 pint sterile water). Cuts on the eyeball, bruises close to the eyes, or persistent discharge should be treated only by a veterinarian.

Heat exhaustion is a serious (and often fatal) problem caused by exposure to extreme heat. Usually it occurs when a thoughtless owner leaves the dog in a closed vehicle without proper shade and ventilation. Even on a day when outside temperatures do not seem excessively high, heat builds up rapidly to an extremely high temperature in a closed vehicle parked in direct sunlight or even in partial shade. Many dogs and young children die each year from being left in an inadequately ventilated vehicle. To prevent such a tragedy, an owner or parent should never leave a dog or child unattended in a vehicle even for a short time.

During hot weather, whenever a dog is taken for a ride in an air-conditioned automobile, the cool air should be reduced gradually when nearing the destination, for the sudden shock of going from cool air to extremely hot temperatures can also result in shock and heat exhaustion.

Symptoms of heat exhaustion include rapid and difficult breathing and near or complete collapse. After removing the victim from the vehicle, first aid treatment consists of sponging cool water over the body to reduce temperature as quickly as possible. Immediate medical treatment is essential in severe cases of heat exhaustion.

Care of the Ailing or Injured Dog

A dog that is seriously ill, requiring surgical treatment, transfusions, or intravenous feeding, must be hospitalized. One requiring less complicated treatment is better cared for at home, but it is essential that the dog be kept in a quiet environment. Preferably his bed should be in a room apart from family activity, yet close at hand, so his condition can be checked frequently. Clean bedding and adequate warmth are essential, as are a constant supply of fresh, cool water, and foods to tempt the appetite.

Special equipment is not ordinarily needed, but the following items will be useful in caring for a sick dog, as well as in giving first aid for injuries:

petroleum jelly	tincture of metaphen
rubbing alcohol	cotton, gauze, and adhesive tape
mineral oil	burn ointment
rectal thermometer	tweezers
hydrogen peroxide	boric acid solution (2%)

If special medication is prescribed, it may be administered in any one of several ways. A pill or small capsule may be concealed in a small piece of meat, which the dog will usually swallow with no problem. A large capsule may be given by holding the dog's mouth open, inserting the capsule as far as possible down the throat, then holding the mouth closed until the dog swallows. Liquid medicine should be measured into a small bottle or test tube. Then, if the corner of the dog's lip is pulled out while the head is tilted upward, the liquid can be poured between the lips and teeth, a small amount at a time. If he refuses to swallow, keeping the dog's head tilted and stroking his throat will usually induce swallowing.

Liquid medication may also be given by use of a hypodermic syringe without a needle. The syringe is slipped into the side of the mouth and over the rise at the back of the tongue, and the medicine is "injected" slowly down the throat. This is especially good for medicine with a bad taste, for the medicine does not touch the taste buds in the front part of the tongue. It also eliminates spills and guarantees that all the medicine goes in.

Foods offered the sick dog should be particularly nutritious and easily digested. Meals should be smaller than usual and offered at more frequent intervals. If the dog is reluctant to eat, offer food he particularly likes and warm it slightly to increase aroma and thus make it more tempting.

The Stone-Age Dog.

A Spotted Dog from India, ``Parent of the modern Coach Dog.''

History of the Genus Canis

The history of man's association with the dog is a fascinating one, extending into the past at least seventy centuries, and involving the entire history of civilized man from the early Stone Age to the present.

The dog, technically a member of the genus *Canis*, belongs to the zoological family group *Canidae*, which also includes such animals as wolves, foxes, jackals, and coyotes. In the past it was generally agreed that the dog resulted from the crossing of various members of the family *Canidae*. Recent findings have amended this theory somewhat, and most authorities now feel the jackal probably has no direct relationship with the dog. Some believe dogs are descended from wolves and foxes, with the wolf the main progenitor. As evidence, they cite the fact that the teeth of the wolf are identical in every detail with those of the dog, whereas the teeth of the jackal are totally different.

Still other authorities insist that the dog always has existed as a separate and distinct animal. This group admits that it is possible for a dog to mate with a fox, coyote, or wolf, but points out that the resulting puppies are unable to breed with each other, although they can breed with stock of the same genus as either parent. Therefore, they insist, it was impossible for a new and distinct genus to have developed from such crossings. They then cite the fact that any dog can be mated with any other dog and the progeny bred among themselves. These researchers point out, too, heritable characteristics that are different in these animals. For instance, the pupil of the eye of the fox is eliptical and vertical, while the pupil is round in the dog, wolf, and coyote. Tails, too, differ considerably, for tails of foxes, coyotes, and wolves always drop behind them, while those of dogs may be carried over the back or straight up.

Much conjecture centers on two wild dog species that still exist—the Dingo of Australia, and the Dhole in India. Similar in appearance, both are reddish in color, both have rather long, slender jaws, both have rounded ears that stand straight up, and both species hunt in packs. Evidence indicates that they had the same ancestors. Yet, today, they live in areas that are more than 4,000 miles apart.

Despite the fact that it is impossible to determine just when the dog first appeared as a distinct species, archeologists have found definite proof that the dog was the first animal domesticated by man. When man lived by tracking, trapping, and killing game, the dog added to the forces through which man discovered and captured the quarry. Man shared his primitive living quarters with the dog, and the two together devoured the prey. Thus, each helped to sustain the life of the other. The dog assisted man, too, by defending the campsite against marauders. As man gradually became civilized, the dog's usefulness was extended to guarding the other animals man domesticated, and, even before the wheel was invented, the dog served as a beast of burden. In fact, archeological findings show that aboriginal peoples of Switzerland and Ireland used the dog for such purposes long before they learned to till the soil.

Cave drawings from the palaeolithic era, which was the earliest part of the Old World Stone Age, include hunting scenes in which a rough, canine-like form is shown alongside huntsmen. One of these drawings is believed to be 50,000 years old, and gives credence to the theory that all dogs are descended from a primitive type ancestor that was neither fox nor wolf.

Archeological findings show that Europeans of the New Stone Age possessed a breed of dogs of wolf-like appearance, and a similar breed has been traced through the successive Bronze Age and Iron Age. Accurate details are not available, though, as to the external appearance of domesticated dogs prior to historic times (roughly four to five thousand years ago).

Early records in Chaldean and Egyptian tombs show that several distinct and well-established dog types had been developed by about 3700 B.C. Similar records show that the early people of the Nile Valley regarded the dog as a god, often burying it as a mummy in special cemeteries and mourning its death.

Some of the early Egyptian dogs had been given names, such as Akna, Tarn, and Abu, and slender dogs of the Greyhound type and a short-legged Terrier type are depicted in drawings found in Egyptian royal tombs that are at least 5,000 years old. The Afghan Hound and the Saluki are shown in drawings of only slightly later times. Another type of ancient Egyptian dog was much heavier and more powerful, with short coat and massive head. These

Bas-relief of Hunters with Nets and Mastiffs. From the walls of Assurbanipal's palace at Nineveh 668-626 B.C. *British Museum.*

probably hunted by scent, as did still another type of Egyptian dog that had a thick furry coat, a tail curled almost flat over the back, and erect "prick" ears.

Early Romans and Greeks mentioned their dogs often in literature, and both made distinctions between those that hunted by sight and those that hunted by scent. The Romans' canine classifications were similar to those we use now. In addition to dogs comparable to the Greek sight and scent hounds, the ancient Romans had Canes *villatici* (housedogs) and Canes *pastorales* (sheepdogs), corresponding to our present-day working dogs.

The dog is mentioned many times in the Old Testament. The first reference, in Genesis, leads some Biblical scholars to assert that man and dog have been companions from the time man was created. And later Biblical references bring an awareness of the diversity in breeds and types existing thousands of years ago.

As civilization advanced, man found new uses for dogs. Some required great size and strength. Others needed less of these characteristics but greater agility and better sight. Still others needed an accentuated sense of smell. As time went on, men kept those puppies that suited specific purposes especially well and bred them together. Through ensuing generations of selective breeding, desirable characteristics appeared with increasing frequency. Dogs used in a particular region for a special purpose gradually became more like each other, yet less like dogs of other areas used for different purposes. Thus were established the foundations for the various breeds we have today.

The American Kennel Club, the leading dog organization in the United States, divides the various breeds into six "Groups," based on similarity of purposes for which they were developed.

"Sporting Dogs" include the Pointers, Setters, Spaniels, and Retrievers that were developed by sportsmen interested in hunting game birds. Most of the Pointers and Setters are of comparatively recent origin. Their development parallels the development of sporting firearms, and most of them evolved in the British Isles. Exceptions are the Weimaraner, which was developed in Germany, and the Vizsla, or Hungarian Pointer, believed to have been developed by the Magyar hordes that swarmed over Central Europe a

Bas-relief of Assyrian Mastiffs hunting wild horses. *British Museum.*

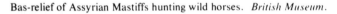

thousand years ago. The Irish were among the first to use Spaniels, though the name indicates that the original stock may have come from Spain. Two Sporting breeds, the American Water Spaniel and the Chesapeake Bay Retriever, were developed entirely in the United States.

"Hounds," among which are Dachshunds, Beagles, Bassets, Harriers, and Foxhounds, are used singly, in pairs, or in packs to "course" (or run) and hunt for rabbits, foxes, and various rodents. But little larger, the Norwegian Elkhound is used in its native country to hunt big game—moose, bear, and deer.

The smaller Hound breeds hunt by scent, while the Irish Wolfhound, Borzoi, Scottish Deerhound, Saluki, and Greyhound hunt by sight. The Whippet, Saluki, and Greyhound are notably fleet of foot, and racing these breeds (particularly the Greyhound) is popular sport.

The Bloodhound is a member of the Hound Group that is known world-wide for its scenting ability. On the other hand, the Basenji is a comparatively rare Hound breed and has the distinction of being the only dog that cannot bark.

"Working Dogs" have the greatest utilitarian value of all modern dogs and contribute to man's welfare in diverse ways. The Boxer, Doberman Pinscher, Rottweiler, German Shepherd, Great Dane, and Giant Schnauzer are often trained to serve as sentries and aid police in patrolling streets. The German Shepherd is especially noted as a guide dog for the blind. The Collie, the various breeds of Sheepdogs, and the two Corgi breeds are known throughout the world for their extraordinary herding ability. And the exploits of the St. Bernard and Newfoundland are legendary, their records for saving lives unsurpassed.

The Siberian Husky, the Samoyed, and the Alaskan Malamute are noted for tremendous strength and stamina. Had it not been for these hardy Northern breeds, the great polar expeditions might never have taken place, for Admiral Byrd used these dogs to reach points inaccessible by other means. Even today, with our jet-age transportation, the Northern breeds provide a more practical means of travel in frigid areas than do modern machines.

"Terriers" derive their name from the Latin *terra*, meaning "earth," for all of the breeds in this Group are fond of burrowing. Terriers hunt by digging into the earth to rout rodents and fur-bearing animals such as badgers, woodchucks, and otters. Some breeds are expected merely to force the animals from their dens in

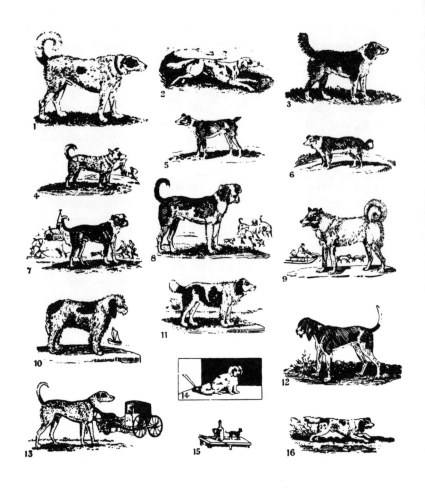

1. The Newfoundland. 2. The English Setter. 3. The Large Water-spaniel. 4. The Terrier. 5. The Cur-dog. 6. The Shepherd's Dog. 7. The Bulldog. 8. The Mastiff. 9. The Greenland Dog. 10. The Rough Water-dog. 11. The Small Water-spaniel. 12. The Old English Hound. 13. The Dalmatian or Coach-dog. 14. The Comporter (very much of a Papillon). 15. "Toy Dog, Bottle, Glass, and Pipe." *From a vignette*. 16. The Springer or Cocker. *From Thomas Bewick's "General History of Quadrupeds" (1790)*.

order that the hunter can complete the capture. Others are expected to find and destroy the prey, either on the surface or under the ground.

Terriers come in a wide variety of sizes, ranging from such large breeds as the Airedale and Kerry Blue to such small ones as the Skye, the Dandie Dinmont, the West Highland White, and the Scottish Terrier. England, Ireland, and Scotland produced most of the Terrier breeds, although the Miniature Schnauzer was developed in Germany.

"Toys," as the term indicates, are small breeds. Although they make little claim to usefulness other than as ideal housepets, Toy dogs develop as much protective instinct as do larger breeds and serve effectively in warning of the approach of strangers.

Origins of the Toys are varied. The Pekingese was developed as the royal dog of China more than two thousand years before the birth of Christ. The Chihuahua, smallest of the Toys, originated in Mexico and is believed to be a descendant of the Techichi, a dog of great religious significance to the Aztecs, while the Italian Greyhound was popular in the days of ancient Pompeii.

"Non-Sporting Dogs" include a number of popular breeds of varying ancestry. The Standard and Miniature Poodles were developed in France for the purpose of retrieving game from water. The Bulldog originated in Great Britain and was bred for the purpose of "baiting" bulls. The Chow Chow apparently originated centuries ago in China, for it is pictured in a bas relief dated to the Han dynasty of about 150 B.C.

The Dalmatian served as a carriage dog in Dalmatia, protecting travelers in bandit-infested regions. The Keeshond, recognized as the national dog of Holland, is believed to have originated in the Arctic or possibly the Sub-Arctic. The Schipperke, sometimes erroneously described as a Dutch dog, originated in the Flemish provinces of Belgium. And the Lhasa Apso came from Tibet, where it is known as "Abso Seng Kye," the "Bark Lion Sentinel Dog."

During the thousands of years that man and dog have been closely associated, a strong affinity has been built up between the two. The dog has more than earned his way as a helper, and his faithful, selfless devotion to man is legendary. The ways in which the dog has proved his intelligence, his courage, and his dependability in situations of stress are amply recorded in the countless tales of canine heroism that highlight the pages of history, both past and present.

Dogs in Woodcuts. (*1st row*) (LEFT) "Maltese dog with shorter hair";
(RIGHT) "Spotted sporting dog trained to catch game"; (*2nd row*) (LEFT)
Sporting white dog; (RIGHT) "Spanish dog with floppy ears": (*3rd row*)
(LEFT) "French dog"; (RIGHT) "Mad dog of Grevinus"; (*4th row*) (LEFT)
Hairy Maltese dog; (RIGHT) "English fighting dog . . . of horrid aspect." *From
Aldrovandus (1637).*

History of the Miniature Pinscher

By Mrs. Carl B. Cass

From archeological studies done by outstanding German scientists, from reports in the archives of the German Pinscher-Schnauzer Klub, and from other original German sources, the following brief history has been compiled.

The Miniature Pinscher is part of the larger German Pinscher family, which belonged to the prehistoric group called *Torfspitzgrupe**, which existed as early as 3000 B. C. Dr. L. Rutimeyer, in recording and identifying the Torfspitz, noted that it appeared in the same form or type even when found in widely different areas. During the late Stone Age, within the Torfspitzgrupe, the Pinscher-type dog was undergoing changes that made it a distinct breed type with unusual features still present in today's Pinschers.

One of the clear-cut traits present in the ancient Pinschers was that of the two opposing size tendencies: one toward the medium to larger size and the other toward the smaller "dwarf" of miniature size. This ancient miniature-sized Pinscher was the forerunner of today's Miniature Pinscher. This answers the question new fanciers often ask: "Is the Miniature Pinscher bred down from the Doberman Pinscher?" The answer is definitely "No." Since ancient times, this Miniature was developing with its natural tendency to smallness in stature.

Not only did the ancient Pinschers appear in two sizes. They also appeared with two different coats: one we shall identify as *wire-coat*** and the other as *smooth-coat*. As late as 1700, breeders still had not done much to separate the two kinds of coats. But when these two coat types finally were separated, the *wire-coated* dogs became known as Schnauzer, Affenpinscher, etc., and the smooths retained the name Pinscher. The small-sized Schnauzer was to become today's Miniature Schnauzer, and the small smooth-coat was to be today's Miniature Pinscher.

*Torf means "turf," *spitz* means "terrier," *grupe* means "group."
***To simplify terminology, *wire-coat* is used to refer to all coats that were not smooth.

Illustrations supplied by v a r i o u s clubs in Germany and reproduced in the volume entitled *Honden Rassen,* by H. A. Graaf Van Bylandt, published in Brussels in September, 1904.

Then a long period of time elapsed which left us little skeletal evidence. Yet, specimens from later historical periods showed that the same tendencies which had identified the Pinscher as a distinct breed had been advancing through the centuries in the same direction—i. e., the narrowing and lengthening of the top skull and the lengthening and gradual molding of the muzzle so that it did not narrow-in so extremely as in some of the other breeds. Richard Strebel, the German painter, searched carefully through the works of the old masters both in paintings and literature and could not find unequivocable likenesses of Pinschers. But it is lucky for our fanciers today that sincere interest had been awakened, for this has given us some evidence of what our Pinschers were like in the eighteenth century and onward.

A few examples of this early evidence in paintings and print may be of interest. One of the earliest typical pictures of Pinschers shows them springing at horses in the painting by the French artist Carl Vernet (1758-1835) entitled *"Le Depart et Le Retour du Chasseur."* The 1836 book by Dr. Reichenbach shows characteristic pictures of both the smooth and the wire Pinscher. And another German writer from the same period, Bumgartz (whose knowledge of the breed was concerned with those from southern Germany), gave a detailed picture of the smooth Pinscher and his characteristics. Some writers from this period were differentiating between the two different types of coats in identifying the dogs. But others would use only the word *Pinscher*. Just one reference to another "Pinscher" (or Terrier, as they are called in England) occurs. German writers mention that black and rust-marked dogs were in existence in England as early as the seventeenth century and were developing the same two size tendencies. It may well be that these are the forerunners of today's *Manchester Terriers* (Toy and Standard sizes).

Until the 1880's, both the wire-coated and the smooth-coated Pinschers had been developing pretty much on their own. Then in 1880, the German Genealogical Register first recorded the breed characteristics of the Pinschers, wire and smooth. In 1895, the German Pinscher-Schnauzer Klub was formed, largely through the efforts of J. Berta, a well-known judge of dogs in Germany. He and other judges insisted that each breed within the Pinscher family must be developed independently so that each breed could be dis-

67

tinctly identified. So the club members started their program of individualizing each breed. This was a difficult task. It was a problem of separating the sizes, of trying to separate the coats which were smooth, or wire, or long and curly, or shaggy and uneven, and of trying to separate the shorter, broader head types with shorter muzzles from those with the longer, narrower ones. So finally the separation was taking place in size, coat, and head type which eventually would give us Miniature Pinschers, Schnauzers in three sizes, Affenpinschers, and other related breeds. For those who are wondering about the place of the Doberman Pinscher in this Pinscher history, the Doberman breed name is attributable to J. Dobermann, who, about 1860 in Thuringia, Germany, crossed a Thuringia Shepherd with the medium-sized Pinscher to give size and stamina to this less favorably endowed Pinscher.

Through the following years, man further "created" this breed, and brought it to the United States, where it won favor. The medium-sized Pinscher still exists in Germany but did not win sufficient interest as a breed to merit exporting it to the United States.

There is a more definite feeling of breed-history when some early dogs are named along with their dates of birth. Some even have show win records. These Miniature Pinschers were registered in the Pinscher-Register and in the Pinscher-Schnauzer Register. The transfer from book to book has left some confusion in registration numbers, but birth dates and descriptions are very clear. *Bijou,* a black with yellow-brown markings, was whelped in March 1879. Owned by August Michel of Berlin, he is listed as winning First at Berlin in 1880. *Marlitt,* owned by Max Hortenstein, was whelped in October of 1884. About 1900, the first chocolate with rust markings, named *Lady,* was registered. The breeding is unknown for *Siergerin Bobby,* whelped at the kennels of Mrs. Doctor Louis Jung. Her *Prinz Liliput,* a black with rust-brown markings, was whelped on March 6, 1900. He won prizes in 1901 and 1902. This *Prinz* and *Lady* (whelped November 28, 1898, purchased from Phil Koch of Frankfurt a. M.) produced many Miniature Pinschers for Mrs. Jung. These are a few evidences of careful breeding and of working together among fanciers from Berlin, Wiesbaden, Nuernberg, Chemnitz, Charlottenburg, Frankfurt, and Sonnenberg—to name only a few places.

What was the aim of most of the Miniature Pinscher breeders of the 1800's? Smaller and still smaller! As one breeder of the 1890's wrote, "The highest ideal . . . they sought was smallness for which they sacrificed everything else." Often the judges at shows had to judge these little dogs in their cages. At other times, the women would hold their beribboned and bejeweled little ones in their arms or even on satin pillows to be judged. The little animals were not allowed to come into contact with the ground. No critical judgment of movement could be made. A judge was almost forced to make his choice in terms of head and smallness. Had such a custom been allowed to continue unchanged, the sturdy, healthy Toy specimens we know today probably would never have been produced.

The change in the method of showing Toy dogs and in breeding aims was fostered to a great extent by early German judges. One judge, J. Berta, led the fight to improve "dwarf"-sized dogs. It was he who insisted that a Toy dog being judged must move on the ground in order to be tested for soundness. Mainly through his efforts, the early-day, degenerated specimens were eliminated. He insisted upon "healthy, well-balanced, tightly-knit specimens with good gait, uniformity in neck and head, correct color markings, and, least of all, diminutiveness." Every step of the way in his battle for his "ideal" Miniature Pinscher, he was harassed by the breeders, who said he "poorly understood Miniature dog affairs." Berta seemed to battle single-handed against the all-powerful Berlin Miniature (Toy) Dog Club. In fact, these breeders of Toy dogs would have banned J. Berta from judging their dogs had they been in a position to do so. But at that time the dog shows were not under the jurisdiction of groups of breeders and exhibitors. They were run by Dog Associations. And the Associations, much to the consternation of the Toy exhibitors, repeatedly assigned J. Berta to judge the Toy dogs. So his influence continued in spite of organized efforts by dog breeders to negate his ideas. Just how small the Miniature Pinscher had previously been is reflected in the fact that judges felt great strides had been made when the Berlin Breed Book listed height as 10¼ inches. In picturing a Miniature Pinscher in 1895, Richard Strebel indicated height at the shoulder of "under 11 inches" as desirable. One breeder of the 1900 era wrote, "The quarrel over the question of size and over the emphasis of abnormal smallness remained." His own conclusion

"Prinzl"

"Puc van Leiden"

"Miss"

"Hansel" and "Gretel"

"Prinz"

was that "the size of the male should not be over 11 inches in height; females, in general, may be somewhat sturdier and may be nearly 12 inches." Yet, as recently as 1931, a German encyclopedia still gave the height of Miniature Pinschers as 10.26 inches. Although the Berlin breeders strove for a more stocky dog with short neck and matching head type, many others were following the aim of more graceful lines.

J. Berta, who had helped formulate many breed Standards, wrote prolifically on the subject of the "ideal Miniature Pinscher." He led the battle for graceful body lines, emphasized the importance of the typical head with strong rather than weak muzzle and stressed the need of all parts to harmonize into a unified picture of good proportions. One of his most exacting demands was that a Miniature Pinscher have what he called a "whole head," not like a "sparrow's beak." He desired a well-developed muzzle which "works itself strongly out of the skull." Breeders who were following the Berta tradition were seeking "a more elongated, well-arched neck and elongated head conformation, minus protruding eyes." How clearly Berta visualized his ideal Miniature Pinscher of the future is seen in the article he wrote for a Frankfurt *Sportblatt* in 1906, which said in part: "I consider as ideal the Miniature Pinscher head which fits with the four-square body, with the strong, upright forequarters, with the sinewy back, with the neck which flows alert and sinewy out of the shoulder and which carries the lines of breeding art; which, as a whole, fits in harmoniously and presents a fitting and aesthetic effect . . . I want a whole head and not merely a skull with a pair of ugly eyes; I want a head with a well-developed muzzle which works itself strongly out of the skull; and if these two, muzzle and skull, fit together to create a head of beautiful lines, then a uniform and harmonious unity is formed, a perfect picture of breeding created." This statement of the requirements of type was so sharp a departure from the Berlin breed characteristics that it caused the Berlin Toy Dog Club to feud openly with Berta and to question his ability to judge Toy dogs.

Fortunately for those who have pride in today's sturdy but elegant and graceful Miniature Pinschers, there were breeders and professionals who had been working along the lines of the ideal set forth by J. Berta and favored by many judges of that period.

Terrier Allemand Nain
ideal

"Mina"

"Comtesse Marie" and "Minnie von
Trautheim"

Ideal Zwerg Pinscher and Maltese

"Boy" and "Fly"

"Mr. John"

One who quickly tried to put into effect the conformation details described by J. Berta was Ernst Kniss of Leipzig. He carefully sought out the most suitable breeding animals and through his careful selection met with outstanding success in producing types which closely paralleled Berta's ideal. He brought out winner after winner. And within a remarkably short span of years, his kennel name of "Klein Paris" was recognized as representing the best in Miniature Pinschers. And his breeding continued to improve. Kniss not only developed the desired characteristics so much needed by the breed at that time—graceful, healthy, and well-knit body lines and well-proportioned head—but in addition to these indispensible qualities, he maintained the smallness of stature. His last star was *Champion Wichtel,* introduced shortly before the outbreak of World War I. In him all of these qualities were combined. He was regarded as the ultimate in perfection of type along with the fact that he stood just under eleven inches in height. From a long line of once well-known blue ribbon winners from Klein Paris and bearing its name were *Dirndl, Heinerle,* and *Gretel.* Thus, Ernst Kniss met the demands of the new breeding order and realized triumph after triumph. But then came World War I and with it the dispersal of these lovely Miniature Pinschers.

Of great significance for the development of the Miniature Pinscher breed was another breeder of the pre-war era who also followed the lines laid down by Berta as to type. He was Georg Mohr, master of the Rheingold Kennels in Wiesbaden. Until this time, the most prominent and most popular color for a Miniature Pinscher had been black with rust (or sometimes yellow) markings. The second color choice was the dark brown, and the least desirable was the red color which is seemingly the most popular color today in the United States. But along with dogs of good type, Georg Mohr specialized in the breeding of reddish-coated dogs. He would exhibit a string of six or more of these dogs at numerous shows, and they would always arouse well-deserved attention wherever they were seen. Some of the most noteworthy to carry the Rheingold banner were his *Wotan, Fasolt, Alberich, Wogelinde,* and *Fafner.* Berta understood the importance of stressing the accomplishments of these two breeders in his reports and writings in such a manner as to stimulate greater interest in them and to mold public opinion in favor of his ideals.

As a result of careful breeding to type and of careful selection by a number of judges, just before World War I the Miniature Pinscher reached a remarkable level of perfection and popularity. It was not uncommon to see this breed predominate in numbers at the various shows. More often than not there would be fifty to sixty specimens of average to excellent quality and uniformity of type to be seen at one show. These have been termed the "Golden Years" for Miniature Pinschers.

The years of World War I marked the beginning of the Miniature Pinscher's decline in Germany. The older breeders who had played such an important part in the breed's development to type had disappeared from the scene. Haphazard, unskilled breeding became rampant. Adding further to the chaos, the older generation of judges who had collaborated in the breed's development and were familiar with the formerly prevailing standards, who had pointed out the defects or superior qualities of stance, head, or size, had lost their influence in the years following the war's end. The new "fledgling judges," no longer chosen by the breed societies, seemed to know very little of the enormous efforts that had gone into the building of the breed. Rapid deterioration ensued.

But a few breeders in the Rhein Provinces and Frankfurt were still striving toward the healthy, stylish ideal. It is to these breeders who carried on the work toward the Berta ideal that the fanciers in the United States owe much—in that it is through them that some of our good early stock arrived in this country. In Frankfurt, the reddish-brown coated variety was predominant in numbers and popularity. Many of the best specimens and the top lines in this area stem from the introduction into the bloodlines of the highly prepotent sire *Ch. Sieger Vom Affentor*. Some of his best progeny, *Afra Vom Kinzdorf, Rheingolds Brilliant,* and *Erlkoenig*, along with the famous sire himself, were exported to Holland, from whence many of their descendants have been sent to the United States. And a top honor winner at the Nuernberg show, *Koenig Heinzelmaenchen*, was shipped to the United States. This was one of many outstanding specimens produced in the kennel of W. Walther in Offenbach. In fact, one of the complaints of the devotees of the breed in Germany at this time was that much of the best Miniature Pinscher stock was being exported, principally to the United States.

74

To these early breeders and to the judges of their day (especially J. Berta), we owe thanks for sending to this country the graceful, healthy, sturdy, four-square, well-balanced small dog with well-modeled head and graceful neck, from which the fanciers have developed the present-day Miniature Pinscher.

It is interesting to compare today's Miniature Pinscher Standard with that of 1905, as described in detail in the following literal translation after the Brockhaus KONVERSATION LEXIKON, 1905:

THE PINSCHER DOG

A truly German breed of dogs which occurs in four types: (1) The smoothhaired pinscher, characterized by a lively, bold carriage and disposition; head and neck carried well up; ears constantly erect and alert; the very short tail stub (these dogs are always docked) curves directly upwards from its base. Of compact body build and standing well up on graceful and rather longish legs; the head somewhat shorter and the skull wider and more arched than in the English Terrier types. The tips of the ears which break over, are always cropped to give them a smarter appearance. Eyes are of medium size and of marked attentive expression. Neck is free of pouches or wattles; well-rounded back* and neck. Thorax full and deep, more flat than convex latterly. Abdominal underlines rising moderately toward the rear; legs clean-boned and straight from every viewpoint. Toes are well arched and foot round and small. Hair short, close and smooth. Color mostly shiny black with yellowish markings. Less desirable coloring is brown with yellow markings. Still less desirable—solid red or yellow. Regarded as serious defects are weak and too extremely pointed nose; overshot or undershot lower jaw; protruding or bulging eyeballs with a tendency to lachrymation; uncropped ears; oversoft hair coating; black spots within yellow markings and any and all white markings.

Other types of the breed are (2) the smoothhaired Miniature Pinscher which with the exception of size and weight must meet all of the qualifications of the standard type, but may have slightly shorter and silkier hair than the standard; (3) the longhaired (wire) Pinscher, of standard size, also called 'ratcatcher'; (4) the miniature longhaired (wire) Pinscher.

*refers to body-width not to backline.

75

Ch. Connie Von Glick, owned by Tom and Avis Flynn.

Ch. Max Tejas von Otho, owned by Miss Mickey Carmichael.

Outstanding Kennels
And Breeders

It is impossible to give complete credit to all of the kennels and breeders that have contributed to the Miniature Pinscher in America. Some are no longer active and it has not been possible to document their contribution. Others have failed to answer numerous inquiries requesting information on their kennel activities. And I am sure that it has not been possible to contact everyone who has been involved. I have listed the kennels alphabetically just for convenience.

Alema Kennels of Mr. and Mrs. Albert Loest produced many outstanding champions, including the famous Ch. Gypsy of Alema. Gypsy produced ten litters totalling forty-one puppies, nineteen of which obtained their championship. This is indeed quite a record. Alema Kennels produced Ch. Tip-Topper of Alema, Ch. Little Buzzard of Alema, Ch. Hot Rod of Alema, and many other champions that appear in the pedigrees of modern-day Pinschers. The Alema strain has certainly helped control size as well as adding many other desirable features to the breed.

Bailes Miniature Pinscher Kennel is owned by Mrs. Boyce Bailes of Albany, Georgia. This kennel was established in May 1959 and has owned or produced more than forty champions in the eight year period following its establishment. The patriarch of the kennel has been Ch. Shieldcrest Cinnamon Toast, a son of Ch. Bel Roc's Dobe v. Enztal. In addition to winning many Groups, the National Specialty, and an all-breed Best in Show, Cinnamon Toast has produced twenty champions. Mrs. Bailes has made an outstanding contribution to the breed and has been an officer of the Miniature Pinscher Club of America—serving as secretary.

Baum's Kennel was established by Mrs. Pearl Baum of Canton, Ohio, in 1947. Using foundation stock acquired from Rochburg and von Enztal lines, Mrs. Baum produced thirty-seven champions, including three Group winners, during her first two decades as a Min-Pin breeder. Her top producing stud, Ch. Baum's Little Klinker, sired seven champions, and her top producing dam, Ch. Baum's Little Chickie, produced seven champion offspring. Mrs.

Baum has used Ch. Bel-Roc's Dobe v. Enztal and the German import, Ch. Bubi Frien Reuchesttadt Rothenburg, as the prime studs in her breeding program. She states that the German import has been helpful in producing short bodies, medium size, and very strong hindquarters, whereas Dobe has produced excellent heads and necks, and has provided the further attribute of elegance.

The Bel-Roc Kennel, owned by Mr. and Mrs. Forest P. Booher of Williamstown, West Virginia, was established in 1951, utilizing von Enztal and Rochsburg as well as Reedlynde bloodlines. This kennel has been noted for famous sires, including Ch. Rusty v. Enztal, Ch. Bel-Roc's Dobe v. Enztal, Ch. Sergeant Fritz v. Enztal, and Bel-Roc's Snicklefritz v. Enztal. All of these dogs are sires of many champions, including some of the top winners of the 1960's. As a matter of fact, it is rather unusual to find a current top winner whose pedigree does not include one of these sires. Mrs. Booher served as secretary of the national club for many years and as president for two years. She has provided a great deal of assistance to many newcomers in the breed.

Birling Kennel, owned by Mr. Lionel Hamilton-Renwick, Upend, N. R. Newmarket, Suffolk, England, has produced some outstanding winners during the past several years. These include Ch. Birling's Painted Lady, Ch. Birling's Wawocan Constellation, Ch. Birling's Bright Star, as well as Ch. Birling's Blissful. Mr. Renwick has utilized American bloodlines very successfully. Those from the Ra Bue and Von Kurt Kennels have blended nicely with the strains already present in the kennel and have made him a top competitor at the English shows.

Bo-Mar Kennel was established by Dr. and Mrs. Buris R. Boshell in Belmont, Massachusetts, in 1956, and subsequently was moved to Birmingham, Alabama (in 1959). The kennel started with a puppy, later to become Ch. Rebel Roc's Cora v. Kurt, who proved to be a top producer. Von Enztal, Von Kurt, and Alema have provided the foundation bloodlines for the Bo-Mar breeding. Top winners include the Best-in-Show winning Bo-Mar's Drummer Boy, Best-in-Show winning Ch. Rebel Roc's Starboarder (a young flashy red sired by Casanova out of Ch. Bo-Mar's Ballet Dancer), and the following Group winners: Ch. Bo-Mar's Ginger Snap, Ch. Bo-Mar's Snicklefritz, Ch. Bo-Mar's Saucy Susan, and Ch. Bo-Mar's Brandy of Jay Mac.

The Cass-Lyne Miniature Pinscher Kennel has been in existence for more than twenty years, although Mrs. Cass has recently discontinued her breeding as she has become more active as a judge. One of her early Min-Pins was La-Roy's Show Boy, purchased from Adam Strauss in Chicago. He is the dog she credits strongly as the producer of the correct head and neck type. In addition, Mrs. Cass used descendants of the Utterback, Baum's, and Snow Fair Kennels. From the latter she purchased Ch. Snow Fair Tommy Tinker, a Toy Group winner. Cass-Lyne bloodlines appear in dogs owned by the Helms of Oklahoma City; the Edward Whartons of Duncan, Oklahoma; the Ed Underhills of Tulsa, Oklahoma; the Baddeleys of California; and the Clinton Craigs of Illinois.

Dr. Henry Celaya was an active breeder and exhibitor of dogs from 1925 through 1950. He was subsequently licensed by The American Kennel Club to judge Terriers, Toys, and the Working Group. Dr. Celaya's dogs were shown by Col. Dick Davis and in addition to Miniature Pinschers, Dr. Celaya exhibited Great Danes, Wires, Scottish and Bull Terriers, and English Setters. In 1938 Dr. Celaya's Miniature Pinscher Ch. Fritz von Arnowtal—American-bred male—went Best in Show at Fort Worth under Judge Lewis Warden. I was told by Dr. Celaya that this was the first American-bred Miniature Pinscher to do so. There were many outstanding dogs at the show, including the famous Boxer, Ch. Dorian von Marienof, as well as some of Mrs. Hoyt's outstanding Poodles. Later on Fritz was Best of Breed and Fourth in the Group at Westminster. In 1940 Ch. Barbelle v. Wurzburger Glockle was imported from Germany by Mrs. Owen West. Later she was purchased by Dr. Celaya. This bitch won several large Groups, including the Chicago International, and she went Best in Show at the Louisville All-Breed Show. When she was bred to King Eric v. Konigsbach, she produced four pups: Ch. Anton v. Wurzbach, Ch. Adolphe v. Wurzbach, Ch. August v. Wurzbach, and Ch. Ann v. Wurzbach. The best of this litter was Ch. Anton, who won over forty Groups and was four times Best in Show. Dr. Celaya states that in his days of exhibiting, top competition in Miniature Pinschers was provided by Mrs. William Bagshaw of Beverly Hills, Dr. Hartman of Detroit, and Mrs. Barnes of Beaumont, Texas. Mrs. Barnes owned the famous Tejas Kennel.

The Craig Hill Kennels were established in 1961 by Clinton R.

Ch. Mudhen Acre's Red Snapper, Best in Show. Owner-breeder-handler, Hank Hearn.

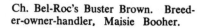

Ch. Bel-Roc's Buster Brown. Breeder-owner-handler, Maisie Booher.

Louisville Kennel Club, Best-in-Show Winner, Ch. Rebel Roc's Starboarder. Breeder, Mrs. E. W. Tipton, Jr. Handler-owner, Dr. Buris R. Boshell. Judge, Mrs. Charles Austin.

Ch. Luddymarie's Halrok's Sport winning Best of Opposite Sex from the Classes at the Putnam, N. Y., Kennel Club Show, July 23, 1966. Judge, Mrs. Emma Stephens.

and Edna Craig, utilizing von Tejas and Baum's as well as Cass-Lyne bloodlines. Ch. Tiny of Craighill has been a mainstay of this kennel. Mr. Craig is an avid sportsman and supports many of the shows in the Midwest. He has made some outstanding wins with a son of Ch. Bo-Mar's Top Skipper—El-Mar's Black Zorro. And one of Zorro's young daughters, Sparkles of Craighill, has become one of the most talked about young bitches in the Midwest.

Dascom Miniature Pinschers, owned by Fiona Mullen, was established in 1956, primarily with von Enztal bloodlines. Mrs. Mullen produced nine champions in eleven litters, including the Group winning Ch. Dascom Danseuse.

Delcrest Miniature Pinschers, owned by Mrs. Della M. Harris, was established in 1963 with animals of the Sanbrook bloodline. Among Mrs. Harris's first six champions was the Group winning Ch. Delcrest Tiki Doll. A top stud in her kennel has been Ch. Karitom's Smoking Sabre, who sired a number of champions. Mrs. Harris travels widely with her Pinschers and provides strong competition at all the shows where she exhibits.

The Eldomar Kennels are owned by Mrs. E. L. Doheny. This kennel did a great deal to popularize the Miniature Pinscher in the past with some very outstanding specimens, including Ch. King Allah von Siegenburg, who sired thirty-eight champions, and Ch. Patzie von Mill-Mass. Patzie's all-time record consisted of twenty-five Best in Show wins and a hundred Toy Group Firsts. She was campaigned to this record by Mr. Porter Washington, who told me that during her career she defeated every top dog of her time in the United States. She also won the Quaker Oats Award every year that she was shown.

Gais Lurons Kennel is owned by Mr. Philippe Pratte of Becanour, Quebec, Canada. This kennel contains Ch. Carwyn's Sonnet, Ch. Carwyn's Yeoman, Carwyn's Pana, Griffwood's Smoking Sabu, and others. Mr. Pratte is a very enthusiastic breeder and is utilizing some of the top studs in the United States.

Griffwood Kennel was established in 1961 by Mr. and Mrs. Thomas B. Griffith, using foundation animals from the Dascom and the Rebel-Roc Kennels. Tom and Ora Griffith, well respected exhibitors, are responsible for the production of some good ones.

Grogg's Kennel was established by Betty I. Grogg in April 1965, utilizing Bel-Roc and Geddesburg lines. Despite the fact that the

Ch. Rebel Roc's Vanguard von Kurt   Ch. Rajah v. Siegenburg

Ch. Surprise of Alema   Ch. Hot Rod of Alema

Ch. King Allah von Siegenburg   Ch. Patzie v. Mill-Mass

kennel is new, it has established some very high ideals in its breeding program.

Happywalk Kennels were established in July 1955 by Carl and June Ann Sharits, using Ch. Baum's Little Betzie, C. D., as the foundation animal. Mr. and Mrs. Sharits have produced a number of champions and emphasize good temperament in their breeding program. They have used Ch. Fern Acres' Double Trouble and have doubled up on Ch. Bel-Roc's Dobe v. Enztal and Ch. King Eric von Konigsberg. In addition, they have brought Ch. Midnight Sun von Haymount into their breeding program. Ch. Happywalk's Cinnamon Bear has done some nice winning on the West Coast.

Hayclose Kennel, owned by Mr. John Stott, Burton on Trent, England, was established in 1957, utilizing Geddesburg and Reedlynde exports as well as some of the progeny of Ch. Dobe v. Enztal. This kennel has produced several champions, and Group as well as Best in Show winners. Top producing dam in the kennel is Davina of Tavey. Mr. Stott recognizes English Ch. Culandhu Para Handy as the top sire in England and states that this dog, bred directly back to the von Enztal lines from the United States, has been the progenitor of nearly all of the major English winners.

Haymount Kennel, owned by Mr. W. A. Van Story, Jr., of Weaverville, North Carolina, was registered with The American Kennel Club in 1941. Early in their breeding program, this kennel utilized Ch. Mitsou de Haelen and Ch. Kama Bitte von Cleinhoehle as well as Ch. Prinz von Marck and Ch. Frigga von de Sangerburg. Subsequently, Ch. Jigger of Geddesburg and Ch. King Allah von Siegenburg were used, along with Ch. King Eric von Konigsbach, to establish the kennel's American bloodlines. Mr. Van Story has a very active breeding program and has produced some unusually promising youngsters. He is especially proud of his all-champion Midnight litter.

Helms Miniature Pinschers had their beginning in May 1963. Established by Maynard and Joyce Helms, this kennel utilized Bailes, Bel-Roc, and Cass-Lyne foundation stock. One of their outstanding youngsters, Ch. Helm's Gunner General, a son of the famous Bel-Roc's Snicklefritz v. Enztal, won the Dallas Miniature Pinscher Specialty and later a Group First. The Helms are serious breeders and are making fine progress with their program.

Houck-Blu-Stone Kennel, owned by the Arnold Houcks of

Naples, Florida, was established in 1958, utilizing Geddesburg bloodlines. The Houcks have bred several champions and in spite of retirement remain very interested in the breed.

Jay-Mac Kennel, owned by Mr. and Mrs. John McNamara of Grand Rapids, Michigan, was established in 1960. Utilizing Ch. Bo-Mar's Drum Song and Ch. Bo-Mar's Blythe Spirit—both of whom have been "dams of the year," the McNamaras produced twelve champions in short order. Their Ch. Bo-Mar's Drum Son of Jay-Mac was a Group winner at eight months of age, and their Ch. Jay-Mac's Eric the Red proved himself steadily as an outstanding winner and sire.

Kaisertan Kennel of Raleigh, North Carolina, was established by Mr. and Mrs. Philip L. Ceglia in 1965, using the Bailes bloodline.

La Roy Kennel, owned by Mr. Adam Strauss, is no longer active in Miniature Pinschers but has contributed immeasurably to the breed and has produced some outstanding Miniature Pinschers that appear in the pedigrees of many of the modern-day winners. This includes the famous Ch. La-Roy's Toe Dancer von Konigsberg.

Lo-Bob Kennels were established by Mr. and Mrs. Robert Waters in 1956. Their first Miniature Pinscher came from the "Of the Hill Kennels" of Miss Michael Carmichael of Tyler, Texas. Twelve champions have been owned or produced by the Lo-Bob Kennels, including the Best-in-Show winner, Int. Ch. Mystery Gal of Lo-Bob. She finished her American championship in three five-point shows and in 1965 was the second top-ranking Min-Pin in Canada. A more recent acquisition at Lo-Bob is Bo-Mar's Highwayman, grandson of the famous Ch. Bel-Roc's Dobe v. Enztal.

Melamac Kennels were established by Pat and Paul Smith. Among their Min-Pins is Ch. Hie Heidi of Geddesburg, who finished with four Majors and was owner handled all the way.

Mel-Kef Miniature Pinscher Kennel was originated in 1948 by Frank and Ann Kaymel of Rochester, New York, who produced Int. Ch. Mel-Kef's Darktown Strutter, as well as other outstanding dogs. After the death of Mr. Kaymel, the Mel-Kef dogs were turned over to Alice Barton of Zephyr, Ontario. Some of the Mel-Kef line still appear in the Golden Circle Dogs of Tommy Gannon and in the bloodlines of the Veroma Kennels owned by Veronica Stabb.

Merry Hill's Kennels were established in 1950 but were not active in exhibiting until 1952. From Greywing's Kennels in Texas came the first Miniature Pinscher for Merry Hill's—Greywing's Hi Steppin Gigolo, a black and tan male who readily finished his championship and then made some outstanding wins. He was joined by Fancy Fair Snow, a small mahogany red bitch from the Snow Fair Kennels, and by Allah's Kismet of Eldomar from the Eldomar Kennels. (The latter was a black and rust bitch sired by the famous Int. Ch. King Allah von Siegenberg.)

When Gigolo was bred to a King Allah daughter owned by the Bebob's Kennels, Merry Hill's took a choice of the litter—Bebob's Black Magic. Black Magic was then bred to Fancy Fair and produced Ch. Happy Fella, Ch. My Fair Maid, Ch. Merry Hill's Fanciful Miss, and Ch. Merry Hill's Fair Maid. Black Magic, bred to Moon's Angel Wing, sired Ch. Merrie Angel, a black and rust bitch who won Best in Show. Then Magic was bred to Haasmor Monobob Tso, who produced Ch. Haasmor Dineh Babe, a Group and Best-in-Show winner.

Merry Hill's consider their most outstanding dogs to be: Dineh Babe, who won Best in Show three times; Ch. Dazan's Mister Bear, who won Best in Show six times and the Group twenty-one times; and Ch. Peniwil's Nuttin But Trash, who won the Group thirty-seven times and Best in Show three times. They have had twenty-nine champions in their kennel, of which twelve have won Toy Groups and five have won Best in Show. The Best-in-Show winners are Ch. Merry Angel of Merry Hills, Ch. Haasmor Dineh Babe, Ch. Merry Hill's Miss Minnie Pin, Ch. Dazan's Mister Bear, and Ch. Peniwil's Nuttin But Trash.

More recently, Ch. Bo-Mar's Fan Dancer and Ch. Rebel Roc's Starboarder have been campaigned by Merry Hill's in collaboration with Dr. Buris R. Boshell of Birmingham, Alabama.

Minnie Rocket Kennel was established by Mrs. Mary Alice Sticklin in 1961, using foundation stock from Airlane's, Bo-Mar, and Fern Acres Kennels. In 1964 Mrs. Sticklin's Ch. Bo-Mar's Drum Call won the Dallas Min-Pin Specialty and was Best of Opposite Sex at both the Chicago and Trenton Specialties. Mrs. Sticklin's Minnie Rocket Gene von Upper, a son of Ch. Bo-Mar's Pepper Upper ex Bo-Mar's Dancing Doll, was Best of Winners from the Puppy Class at the 1967 Chicago Specialty.

Murphy Kennels are owned by Mr. and Mrs. Leo J. Murphy of

Ch. Tip Topper of Alema, January 27, 1957. Owner, Florence Dendy. Handler, Clara Alford. Breeder, Alema Kennels.

Ch. Rebel Roc's Cover Girl at Raleigh, March 24, 1962. Owner, Mr. H. H. Heming.

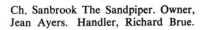

Ch. Sanbrook The Sandpiper. Owner, Jean Ayers. Handler, Richard Brue.

Ch. Rebel Roc's Living Doll, Best in Show at Chattanooga under Mr. Rickle. Handler, Mr. E. W. Tipton, Jr. Owner, Mrs. E. W. Tipton, Jr

Indianapolis, Indiana. The Murphys have been interested in both conformation and obedience, having trained and shown Ch. Hans von Tejas to his U. D. degree. Hans was the sire of the Murphy's Ch. Tim Tam, a winner of three Groups. The Murphys also own Ch. Susie Q, who won a Group. In addition to the Tejas bloodlines, the Murphys purchased Ch. Rebel Roc's Ballerina von Kurt and have done some excellent winning as well as producing with her.

"Of the Hill" Kennels were established by Miss Michael Carmichael in 1948. Miss Carmichael produced twelve champions, six Group winners, and one Best-in-Show winner—Ch. Max Tejas von Otho. Miss Carmichael was a young lady of many talents. She was an animal fancier, a WASP pilot in World War II, and a noted sculptress. Her Sir Ius of the Hill memorial trophy, given to the Dallas Min-Pin Club, is a memento very much treasured by those who have been fortunate enough to win it. "Mickey" was active in establishing the Dallas Miniature Pinscher Club.

"Of North Lane" Kennels were established in 1951 by Mrs. Pat Thurman, utilizing Alema and Siegenburg bloodlines. Mrs. Thurman has not had an extensive breeding program but has been very helpful to many breeders and exhibitors in her area.

Primrose House Kennels, owned by Mrs. Jimmy R. Primm, were established in 1961 utilizing Veroma, Ra-Bue, and Alema bloodlines. Mrs. Primm has produced a number of champions and has an active breeding program.

Ra-Bue Kennels were owned by Mrs. Beulah Cook, and several good ones were produced there while Mrs. Cooke was active in the breed. From Adam Strauss, Mrs. Cooke purchased Ericka v. Konigsberg, who was out of a La-Roy bitch and was sired by Mickey Carmichael's Ch. Sir Ius of the Hill. Ericka was bred back to Ch. La-Roy's Toe Dancer to produce many of Mrs. Cooke's top champions.

Rebel Roc dogs have done a great deal to publicize the Miniature Pinscher during the past several years, for Rebel Roc has had some really outstanding winners. At the head of the list is Ch. Rebel Roc's Casanova von Kurt, winner of seventy-five Best-in-Show awards and innumerable Toy Groups. Other Group winners are Ch. Rebel Roc's Yo Yo, Ch. Rebel Roc's Vanguard von Kurt, Ch. Rebel Roc's Jackpot, Ch. Rebel Roc's Fiesta von Kurt, Ch. Rebel Roc's Living Doll, and Ch. Rebel Roc's Starboarder. The latter three dogs were all Best-in-Show winners as well. Foundation

Ch. Sanbrook Star Topaz. Owner, R. A. Brue. Breeder, Ann Dutton.

Ch. Snow Fair Tommy Tinker. Owner, Mrs. Carl B. Cass.

Int. Ch. Mystery Gal of Lo-Bob. Breeder-owner, Mr. Robert Waters.

stock for Rebel Roc came from the Bel-Roc Kennels of Williamstown, West Virginia.

Reh-Mont Miniature Pinschers were established in 1953 by Harmon and Dixie Montgomery of Evansville, Indiana. The Montgomerys have used the La-Roy, Alema, von Enztal, Bo-Mar, and Rebel Roc bloodlines and have produced several champions and Group winners.

Reel Kennels were owned by Mark Reel of Illinois. At one time Mr. Reel campaigned some top specimens, and he still maintains an active interest in the breed, although he is not an active breeder. Mr. Reel was the first judge of the Sweepstakes held by the National Specialty in Chicago.

Ric-Lor's Kennel was established by Claire Panichi in 1958, utilizing Rochsburg, La-Roy, Rebel Roc, and Woodlands bloodlines. Claire produced Ch. Ric-Lor's Just Mimi, who won the Maryland Specialty in 1966, having been Best of Winners from the Bred-by-Exhibitor Class at the Trenton Specialty.

Rochsburg Kennels, owned by Dr. Frank W. and Mrs. Blanche Hartman, produced eighty-seven champions of record. No longer active in the breed, the influence of the Rochsburg Kennels remains very dominant in the pedigrees of the modern-day Miniature Pinscher.

Roy-Bee's Min Pins were established in 1951 by Roy C. and Ethel R. Berry of Dallas, Texas, utilizing Alema and Mill-Mass bloodlines. The Berrys have produced several champions, including the Best-in-Show winner Roy Bee's Marck von Akers.

Sanbrook Kennels, owned by Mrs. Ann Dutton and Camille Robertson of Hollywood, Florida, finished their first homebred champion in 1961 and garnered some thirty additional champions in the ensuing six years. Group winners produced by Sanbrook include Ch. Sanbrook Sunbeam for Bailes, Ch. Sanbrook Star Topaz, Ch. Sanbrook Sentry von Spritelee, and Ch. Sanbrook Showoff. Sanbrook utilized the Group-winning bitch, Ch. Mudhen Acres Happy Heart, and the Best-in-Show winning stud, Ch. Mudhen Acres Red Snapper, very prominently in their breeding program. Other top winning Sanbrook dogs are Ch. Barpin Coral, C. D. X., Ch. Sanbrook Scarlet von Enztal, Ch. Sanbrook Sisterdoll, and Ch. Sanbrook Stolen Kiss. Ch. Midnight Sun von Haymount and Bel-Roc's Juno von Enztal have had a prominent part as studs in the breeding program. Sanbrook Kennels consistently come up with some good pups each year.

Sandyhill Kennels of Sebastopol, California, were established in 1956 by Florence and Irene Rigby and Zoe Shurtleff, utilizing von Enztal, Geddesburg, Bretelheim, Konigsbach, Konigsberg, and Siegenburg bloodlines. This kennel has produced a number of champions, including one Group winner, and is making sincere efforts to improve the breed.

Scheuring Kennels are owned by Miss Dorothy E. Wilkinson of Chesapeake, Virginia. The kennels originated in 1961 with Ch. Princess Prissie Anni, who not only finished her championship in great style with a Group First in 1962, but also went ahead to complete her C. D. X. in 1966. Katrina von Scheuring finished her Utility degree in 1959. Mrs. Wilkinson has outlined an excellent breeding program and has used some of the top studs in the country in her breeding, including Casanova, Cinnamon Toast, and Sentry. From the Little Daddy litter came Ch. Scheuring's Mischief Maker and from the Cinnamon Toast litter, Ch. Scheuring's Sassy Susanna.

Siegenburg Kennel's suffix was granted by The American Kennel Club to Capt. and Mrs. Ary C. Berry, on December 15, 1949. Of the outstanding dogs produced by these breeders, some of the more prominent are: Ch. Rajah von Siegenburg, who was campaigned in the name of Canyon Crest Kennel; Ch. King Allah von Siegenburg, campaigned by Mrs. Peggy Doheny and handled by Porter Washington; Ch. Cherry von Siegenburg and Ch. Max von Siegenburg, campaigned by Mr. Anton Korbell; and Ch. Rajah von Siegenburg, who was campaigned to his championship by Capt. Berry. Rajah established quite a record, winning three consecutive Toy Groups in three days, attaining fourteen points from the Open Class. In his fourth show in five days, he scored four points, totalling eighteen points in a five-day period. Siegenburg bloodlines still figure prominently in the pedigrees of many of our current winners.

Spritelee Kennels, owned by William H. and Ruby M. Lee of Fort Worth, Texas, were established in 1959, utilizing Bel-Roc, Alema, Veroma, Rochsburg, and Siegenburg bloodlines. Spritelee Kennels have produced a number of champions, including four Group winners and two Best-in-Show winners, the latter being Ch. Spritelee's Reddy Teddy von Bimbo and Ch. Spritelee's Dagmar.

Dagmar is now owned by Richard Brue of New Orleans, Louisiana. In spite of moving about the country because of Bill's particular line of work, the Lees continue to come up with good ones.

Sta-Rite Kennels, which were owned by Mrs. Hall (who later merged with Mrs. Cooke of Ra-Bue Kennels), left quite a mark on the breed. Sta-Rite obtained Bel-Roc's Dinah von Enztal, bred her to Ch. Eldomar's Sentry, and produced the famous sire, Ch. Baron Anthony von Meyer, who later produced the outstanding winner of all time—Ch. Rebel Roc's Casanova von Kurt.

Stormcrest Kennels were established by Mrs. Florence Dendy of Marietta, Georgia. Florence obtained Ch. Tip Topper of Alema from Alema Kennels, campaigned him to his championship, and then utilized him as the top stud in her kennel. An outstanding sire, Tip Topper was also a wonderful showman, with many breed and Group wins. Other Group winners from the Stormcrest Kennels include Ch. Stormcrest Widget, Ch. Rebel Roc's Jupiter von Kurt, and Ch. Stormcrest Bright Flame, dam of the Best-in-Show winning Ch. Shieldcrest Cinnamon Toast.

Suboru Kennels, owned by Bob and Sue Russell of Scranton, Kansas, were established in 1961 using Spritelee and Cass-Lyne foundation stock. The Russells work very closely with Bill and Ruby Lee, of Spritelee fame, in their breeding program.

Veroma Kennels were established in 1946 by Veronica M. Stabb, using Hilgerville, Hanover, Mel-Kef, Golden Circle, and La-Roy bloodlines for foundation stock. Veroma has produced many champions, and Group winners as well.

Von Glick Kennels, owned by Avis and Tom Flynn of Dallas, Texas, have produced a number of champions, including some Group winners. They have used the Alema, La-Roy, and Siegenburg bloodlines in their foundation stock. Their litter-mate champions, Haldee and Honeybun von Glick, have kept these exhibitors in the winners circle frequently during the past two or three years. Sired by Ch. Bo-Mar's Drummer Boy, this outstanding pair of Miniature Pinscher champions is out of Ch. Connie von Glick.

Ch. Riccochet Romance of Alema. Owner, Kirven Griffin.

Ch. Princess Prissie Anni completing her championship at Tidewater Kennel Club, Norfolk, Virginia, November 11, 1962.

Ch. Rebel Roc's Yo Yo, Best of Opposite Sex, 1963 Miniature Pinscher Club of America Specialty. Owner, Mrs. E. W. Tipton, Jr.

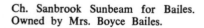

Ch. Sanbrook Sunbeam for Bailes. Owned by Mrs. Boyce Bailes.

Outstanding Sires and Dams

The modern Miniature Pinscher, in my way of thinking, has been influenced more by three sires than by all of the others put together. These three are: first, Ch. Bel-Roc's Dobe v. Enztal; second, Ch. Baron Von Anthony v. Meyer; and third, Ch. Mudhen's Acre Red Snapper.

Grand-progeny or progeny of the famous Ch. Bel-Roc's Dobe v. Enztal have formed the foundation stock for many of the present-day kennels. A Dobe daughter, Ch. Bel-Roc's Sugar v. Enztal, was the foundation bitch for the famous Rebel Roc Kennel; for years, a Dobe son, Ch. Shieldcrest's Cinnamon Toast has been the prime stud of the Bailes' breeding program; and a Dobe grandson, Bel-Roc's Juno v. Enztal, has been a significant contributor to the Sanbrook's breeding. Furthermore, Dobe progeny and grand-progeny produced in the Bel-Roc Kennels have served as foundation animals for many new breeders throughout the country. Gingersnap, a Dobe daughter, was our first homebred champion and Group winner; and Ch. Bo-Mar's Pepper Pot v. Enztal, a Dobe son, is adding champions each year to his long list of winning progeny.

Dobe certainly is a prepotent sire, and it has been of interest to see his traits passed along. He is the sire of Ch. Sergeant Fritz v. Enztal, who sired the famous producer Bel-Roc's Snicklefritz v. Enztal. From the latter came our first Best-in-Show winner, Ch. Bo-Mar's Drummer Boy, who, in spite of very limited use at stud, produced five Group winners in a single year. Two of the five—Ch. Bo-Mar's Brandy of Jay-Mac and Ch. Bo-Mar's Drum Son of Jay-Mac—have already proven that they possess the ability to pass along the desirable traits that started out with Dobe. The 1968 National Sweepstakes winner was a son of Brandy.

Dobe produced the two Best-in-Show winners, Ch. Bel-Roc's Sugar v. Enztal and Ch. Shieldcrest's Cinnamon Toast, and I believe he and his son Fritz and his son Cinnamon Toast are Specialty Show winners as well.

The Dobe traits include elegance, showmanship, and a racy appearance similar to that of a thoroughbred horse.

Ch. Baron Von Anthony v. Meyer stands in rather marked contrast to Dobe. He was more cobby, shorter of leg and neck, and by no means had the elegance of Dobe. When bred to a Dobe granddaughter, Rolling Green's Sparkle, he produced the famous Rebel Roc's Casanova v. Kurt, which would have established him as a great sire even if he had done nothing else whatsoever. Several repeat breedings of "Sparkle" to "Tony," however, continued to produce champions of good quality. And, just as important, if not more so, has been the finding of many breeders that blending a bit of the "Tony" with a fairly large amount of Dobe has resulted in the appearance of a good, sound, medium-sized, elegant Miniature Pinscher. Furthermore, Baron Anthony v. Meyer adds brisket, which has not always been present in the Dobe line. And in addition, good appetite and beautiful, shiny, mahogany red coats frequently result when Baron Anthony is strongly represented in the pedigree.

Number three—Mudhen Acre's Red Snapper—was himself a very sound, elegant little dog. He was bred and owned by the late Hank and Muddy Hearn and later became the property of the Sanbrook Kennels. It is felt by many that Red Snapper added a great deal in strengthening the rear of the Miniature Pinscher. And, although it is not clear when you look at the first part of his pedigree, he is actually a well line-bred dog going back very strongly to the famous Ch. King Eric v. Konigsbach, sire of thirty-six champions. It is of interest that Ch. Midnight Sun v. Haymount and Ch. Sanbrook Sentry v. Spritelee are rather heavily line bred in the Snapper line. Furthermore, a great producing bitch, Rolling Green's Sparkle, dam of twenty champions, is a Snapper daughter out of a Dobe daughter. And one of our most consistent producers is Bo-Mar's Sassy v. Enztal, a Snapper daughter out of a "Tony" daughter.

Ch. King Allah v. Siegenburg has produced a large number of champion offspring (thirty-eight or thirty-nine) and certainly has made a contribution to the breed. Furthermore, Geddesburg champions (including Ch. Gem of Geddesburg), and Alema champions (including Ch. Little Buzzard, Ch. Tip Topper, and many others) have made a definite contribution to the breed.

In more recent years, Ch. Rebel Roc's Casanova v. Kurt, sire of forty champions, Bel-Roc's Snicklefritz v. Enztal, Ch. Rebel Roc's Vanguard, and Ch. Jupiter v. Kurt, Ch. Shieldcrest's Cinnamon Toast (sire of twenty champions), Ch. Sanbrook's Sentry v. Spritelee, Ch. Midnight Sun v. Haymount, and Ch. Bo-Mar's Drummer Boy have contributed significantly to the breed. Bel-Roc's Snicklefritz is the sire of the Best-in-Show winning Champions Bo-Mar's Drummer Boy and Tiny Tiger of Hei Dan, and the Group winning Helms Gunner General.

It is extremely important to realize that the dam is just as important as the sire, if not more so. Two of the most famous dams have been the great producing Ch. Gypsy of Alema, dam of nineteen champions, and Rolling Green's Sparkle, dam of twenty champions. In more recent years, Ch. Rebel-Roc's Cora v. Kurt, Ch. Bo-Mar's Ebony Belle, Ch. Bo-Mar's Drum Song, Ch. Bo-Mar's Blythe Spirit, Bo-Mar's Sassy v. Enztal, Ch. Cass-Lyne's Tinker Teri Dab, and Bel-Roc's Krissie v. Enztal have proven to be outstanding producers.

By necessity, I have discussed primarily the sires that have been prominent in recent years. This is not to decry the influence of the old time greats, but specific, objective information has been difficult to accumulate. Certainly one must include the great Ch. King Eric v. Konigsbach, bred by Mrs. Eunice Wentker. King Eric figures prominently in the pedigrees of many of the modern youngsters, as does Ch. La-Roy's Toe Dancer v. Konigsberg, who was sired by Ch. Swantz v. Rochsburg.

Ch. Prinz v. Marck, Ch. Prinz v. Enztal, Ch. Jigger of Geddesburg, Ch. Marck v. Mill-Mass, Ch. Rusty v. Enztal, Sir Socko of Whitecourt, Tejas Trojan, and Ch. King of Hearts of Geddesburg are also sires of note.

Winslow Homer's "High Tide," painted in 1870 at Manchester-by-the-Sea, Massachusetts.

Ch. Bo-Mar's Snicklefritz at Albany Kennel Club Show, October, 1967. Handler, Jane Kamp Forsythe. Owners, Mr. and Mrs. W. T. Tolbert. Breeder, Dr. Buris R. Boshell.

Ch. Bo-Mar's Brandy. Owners, Mrs. M. Pym and Dr. B. R. Boshell. Judge, Joseph Faizel. Handler, J. Kay.

Ch. Halrok Happy Hussy, Best of Breed at Putnam Kennel Club Show. Breeder-owner-handler, Miss Vera Halpin. Judge, Mrs. Emma Stephens.

Ch. Bailes Cinni Penny winning her first Major from the Puppy Class. Judge, Louis J. Murr. Handler, Joe Gregory. Owner, Mrs. Boyce Bailes.

Manners for the Family Dog

Although each dog has personality quirks and idiosyncrasies that set him apart as an individual, dogs in general have two characteristics that can be utilized to advantage in training. The first is the dog's strong desire to please, which has been built up through centuries of association with man. The second lies in the innate quality of the dog's mentality. It has been proved conclusively that while dogs have reasoning power, their learning ability is based on a direct association of cause and effect, so that they willingly repeat acts that bring pleasant results and discontinue acts that bring unpleasant results. Hence, to take fullest advantage of a dog's abilities, the trainer must make sure the dog understands a command, and then reward him when he obeys and correct him when he does wrong.

Commands should be as short as possible and should be repeated in the same way, day after day. Saying ''Heel,'' one day, and ''Come here and heel,'' the next will confuse the dog. *Heel, sit, stand, stay, down,* and *come* are standard terminology, and are preferable for a dog that may later be given advanced training.

Tone of voice is important, too. For instance, a coaxing tone helps cajole a young puppy into trying something new. Once an exercise is mastered, commands given in a firm, matter-of-fact voice give the dog confidence in his own ability. Praise, expressed in an exuberant tone, will tell the dog quite clearly that he has earned his master's approval. On the other hand, a firm ''No'' indicates with equal clarity that he has done wrong.

Rewards for good performance may consist simply of praising lavishly and petting the dog, although many professional trainers use bits of food as rewards. Tidbits are effective only if the dog is hungry, of course. And if you smoke, you must be sure to wash your hands before each training session, for the odor of nicotine is repulsive to dogs. On the hands of a heavy smoker, the odor of nicotine may be so strong that the dog is unable to smell the tidbit.

Correction for wrong-doing should be limited to repeating ''No,'' in a scolding tone of voice or to confining the dog to his bed. Spanking or striking the dog is taboo—particularly using sticks, which might cause injury, but the hand should never be used either. For field training as well as some obedience work, the hand is used to signal the dog. Dogs that have been punished by slapping have a tendency to cringe whenever they see a hand raised and consequently do not respond promptly when the owner's intent is not to punish but to signal.

Some trainers recommend correcting the dog by whacking him with a rolled-up newspaper. The idea is that the newspaper will not injure the dog but that the resulting noise will condition the dog to avoid repeating the act that seemingly caused the noise. Many authorities object to this type of correction, for it may result in the dog's becoming "noise-shy"—a decided disadvantage with show dogs which must maintain poise in adverse, often noisy, situations. "Noise-shyness" is also an unfortunate reaction in field dogs, since it may lead to gun-shyness.

To be effective, correction must be administered immediately, so that in the dog's mind there is a direct connection between his act and the correction. You can make voice corrections under almost any circumstances, but you must never call the dog to you and then correct him, or he will associate the correction with the fact that he has come and will become reluctant to respond. If the dog is at a distance and doing something he shouldn't, go to him and scold him while he is still involved in wrong-doing. If this is impossible, ignore the offense until he repeats it. Then correct him properly.

Especially while a dog is young, he should be watched closely and stopped before he gets into mischief. All dogs need to do a certain amount of chewing, so to prevent your puppy's chewing something you value, provide him with his own balls and toys. Never allow him to chew cast-off slippers and then expect him to differentiate between cast-off items and those you value. Nylon stockings, wooden articles, and various other items may cause intestinal obstructions if the dog chews and swallows them, and death may result. Rubber and plastic toys may also be harmful if they are of types the dog can bite through or chew into pieces and then swallow. So it is essential that the dog be permitted to chew only on bones or toys he cannot chew up and swallow.

Serious training for obedience should not be started until a dog is a year old. But basic training in house manners should begin the day the puppy enters his new home. A puppy should never be given the run of the house but should be confined to a box or small pen except for play periods when you can devote full attention to him. The first thing to teach the dog is his name, so that whenever he hears it, he will immediately come to attention. Whenever you are near his box, talk to him, using his name repeatedly. During play periods, talk to him, pet him, and handle him, for he must be conditioned so he will not object to being handled by a veterinarian, show judge, or family friend. As the dog investigates his surroundings, watch him carefully and if he tries something he shouldn't, reprimand him with a scolding "No!" If he repeats the offense, scold him and confine him to his box, then praise him. Discipline must be prompt, consistent, and always followed with praise. Never tease the dog, and never allow others to do so. Kindness and understanding are essential to a pleasant, mutually rewarding relationship.

When the puppy is two to three months old, secure a flat, narrow leather collar and have him start wearing it (never use a harness, which will encourage tugging and pulling). After a week or so, attach a light leather lead to the collar during play sessions and let the puppy walk around, dragging the lead behind him. Then start holding the end of the lead and coaxing the puppy to come to you. He will then be fully accustomed to collar and lead when you start taking him outside while he is being housebroken.

Housebreaking can be accomplished in a matter of approximately two weeks provided you wait until the dog is mature enough to have some control over bodily functions. This is usually at about four months. Until that time, the puppy should spend most of his day confined to his penned area, with the floor covered with several thicknesses of newspapers so that he may relieve himself when necessary without damage to floors.

Either of two methods works well in housebreaking—the choice depending upon where you live. If you live in a house with a readily accessible yard, you will probably want to train the puppy from the beginning to go outdoors. If you live in an apartment without easy access to a yard, you may decide to train him first to relieve himself on newspapers and then when he has learned control, to teach the puppy to go outdoors.

If you decide to train the puppy by taking him outdoors, arrange some means of confining him indoors where you can watch him closely—in a small penned area, or tied to a short lead (five or six feet). Dogs are naturally clean animals, reluctant to soil their quarters, and confining the puppy to a limited area will encourage him to avoid making a mess.

A young puppy must be taken out often, so watch your puppy closely and if he indicates he is about to relieve himself, take him out at once. If he has an accident, scold him and take him out so he will associate the act of going outside with the need to relieve himself. Always take the puppy out within an hour after meals—preferably to the same place each time—and make sure he relieves himself before you return him to the house. Restrict his water for two hours before bedtime and take him out just before you retire for the night. When you wake in the morning, take him out again.

For paper training, set aside a particular room and cover a large area of the floor with several thicknesses of newspapers. Confine the dog on a short leash and each time he relieves himself, remove the soiled papers and replace them with clean ones.

As his control increases, gradually decrease the paper area, leaving part of the floor bare. If he uses the bare floor, scold him mildly and put him on the papers, letting him know that there is where he is to relieve himself. As he comes to understand the idea, increase the bare area until papers cover only space equal to approximately two full newspaper sheets. Keep him using the papers, but begin taking him out on a leash at the times of day that he habitually relieves himself. Watch him closely when he is indoors and at the first sign that he needs to go, take him outdoors. With this method too, restrict the puppy's water for two hours before bedtime, but if necessary, permit him to use the papers before you retire for the night.

Using either method, the puppy will be housebroken in an amazingly short time. Once he has learned control he will need to relieve himself only four or five times a day.

Informal obedience training, started at the age of about six to eight months, will provide a good background for any advanced training you may decide to give your dog later. The collar most effective for training is the metal chain-link variety. The correct size for your dog will be about one inch longer than the measurement around the largest part of his head. The chain must be slipped through one of the rings so the collar forms a loop. The collar should be put on with the loose ring at the right of the dog's neck, the chain attached to it coming over the neck and through the holding ring, rather than under the neck. Since the dog is to be at your left for most of the training, this makes the collar most effective.

The leash should be attached to the loose ring, and should be either webbing or leather, six feet long and a half inch to a full inch

Chain-link collar. The collar should be removed whenever the dog is not under your immediate supervision, for many dogs have met death by strangulation when a collar was left on and became entangled in some object.

wide. When you want your dog's attention, or wish to correct him, give a light, quick pull on the leash, which will momentarily tighten the collar about the neck. Release the pressure instantly, and the correction will have been made. If the puppy is already accustomed to a leather collar, he will adjust easily to the training collar. But before you start training sessions, practice walking with the dog until he responds readily when you increase tension on the leash.

Set aside a period of fifteen minutes, once or twice a day, for regular training sessions, and train in a place where there will be no distractions. Teach only one exercise at a time, making sure the dog has mastered it before going on to another. It will probably take at least a week for the dog to master each exercise. As training progresses, start each session by reviewing exercises the dog has already learned, then go on to the new exercise for a period of concerted practice. When discipline is required, make the correction immediately, and always praise the dog after corrections as well as when he obeys promptly. During each session stick strictly to business. Afterwards, take time to play with the dog.

The first exercise to teach is heeling. Have the dog at your left and hold the leash as shown in the illustration on the preceding page. Start walking, and just as you put your foot forward for the first step, say your dog's name to get his attention, followed by the command, "Heel!" Simultaneously, pull on the leash lightly. As you walk, try to keep the dog at your left side, with his head alongside your left leg. Pull on the leash as necessary to urge him forward or back, to right or left, but keep him in position. Each time you pull on the leash, say "Heel!" and praise the dog lavishly. When the dog heels properly in a straight line, start making circles, turning corners, etc.

Once the dog has learned to heel well, start teaching the "sit." Each time you stop while heeling, command "Sit!" The dog will be at your left, so use your left hand to press on his rear and guide him to a sitting position, while you use the leash in your right hand to keep his head up. Hold him in position for a few moments while you praise him, then give the command to heel. Walk a few steps, stop, and repeat the procedure. Before long he will automatically sit whenever you stop. You can then teach the dog to "sit" from any position.

When the dog will sit on command without correction, he is ready to learn to stay until you release him. Simply sit him, command "Stay!" and hold him in position for perhaps half a minute, repeating "Stay," if he attempts to stand. You can release him by saying "O.K." Gradually increase the time until he will stay on command for three or four minutes.

The "stand-stay" should also be taught when the dog is on leash. While you are heeling, stop and give the command "Stand!" Keep the dog from sitting by quickly placing your left arm under him, immediately in front of his right hind leg. If he continues to try to sit, don't scold him but start up again with the heel command, walk a few steps, and stop again, repeating the stand command and preventing the dog from sitting. Once the dog has mastered the stand, teach him to stay by holding him in position and repeating the word "Stay!"

The "down stay" will prove beneficial in many situations, but especially if you wish to take your dog in the car without confining him to a crate. To teach the "down," have the dog sitting at your side with collar and leash on. If he is a large dog, step forward with the leash in your hand and turn so you face him. Let the leash touch the floor, then step over it with your right foot so it is under the instep of your shoe. Grasping the leash low down with both hands, slowly pull up, saying, "Down!" Hold the leash taut until the dog goes down. Once he responds well, teach the dog to stay in the down position (the down-stay), using the same method as for the sit- and stand-stays.

To teach small dogs the "down," another method may be used. Have the dog sit at your side, then kneel beside him. Reach across his back with your left arm, and take hold of his left front leg close to the body. At the same time, with your right hand take hold of his right front leg close to his body. As you command "Down!" gently lift the legs and place the dog in the down position. Release your hold on his legs and slide your left hand onto his back, repeating, "Down, stay," while keeping him in position.

The "come" is taught when the dog is on leash and heeling. Simply walk along, then suddenly take a step backward, saying "Come!" Pull the leash as you give the command and the dog will turn and follow you. Continue walking backward, repeatedly saying "Come," and tightening the leash if necessary.

Once the dog has mastered the exercises while on leash, try taking the leash off and going through the same routine, beginning with the heeling exercise. If the dog doesn't respond promptly, he needs review with the leash on. But patience and persistence will be rewarded, for you will have a dog you can trust to respond promptly under all conditions.

Even after they are well trained, dogs sometimes develop bad habits that are hard to break. Jumping on people is a common habit, and all members of the family must assist if it is to be broken. If the dog is a large or medium breed, take a step forward and raise your knee just as he starts to jump on you. As your knee strikes the dog's chest, command "Down!" in a scolding voice. When a small dog jumps on you, take both front paws in your hands, and, while talking in a pleasant tone of voice, step on the dog's back feet just hard enough to hurt them slightly. With either method the dog is taken by surprise and doesn't associate the discomfort with the person causing it.

Occasionally a dog may be too chummy with guests who don't care for dogs. If the dog has had obedience training, simply command "Come!" When he responds, have him sit beside you.

Excessive barking is likely to bring complaints from neighbors, and persistent efforts may be needed to subdue a dog that barks without provocation. To correct the habit, you must be close to the dog when he starts barking. Encircle his muzzle with both hands, hold his mouth shut, and command "Quiet!" in a firm voice. He should soon learn to respond so you can control him simply by giving the command.

Sniffing other dogs is an annoying habit. If the dog is off leash and sniffs other dogs, ignoring your commands to come, he needs

Benching area at Westminster Kennel Club Show.

to review the lessons on basic behavior. When the dog is on leash, scold him, then pull on the leash, command "Heel," and walk away from the other dog.

A well-trained dog will be no problem if you decide to take him with you when you travel. No matter how well he responds, however, he should never be permitted off leash when you walk him in a strange area. Distractions will be more tempting, and there will be more chance of his being attacked by other dogs. So whenever the dog travels with you, take his leash along—and use it.

Judging for Best in Show at Westminster Kennel Club Show.

Show Competition

Centuries ago, it was common practice to hold agricultural fairs in conjunction with spring and fall religious festivals, and to these gatherings, cattle, dogs, and other livestock were brought for exchange. As time went on, it became customary to provide entertainment, too. Dogs often participated in such sporting events as bull baiting, bear baiting, and ratting. Then the dog that exhibited the greatest skill in the arena was also the one that brought the highest price when time came for barter or sale. Today, these fairs seem a far cry from our highly organized bench shows and field trials. But they were the forerunners of modern dog shows and played an important role in shaping the development of purebred dogs.

The first organized dog show was held at Newcastle, England, in 1859. Later that same year, a show was held at Birmingham. At both shows dogs were divided into four classes and only Pointers and Setters were entered. In 1860, the first dog show in Germany was held at Apoldo, where nearly one hundred dogs were exhibited and entries were divided into six groups. Interest expanded rapidly, and by the time the Paris Exhibition was held in 1878, the dog show was a fixture of international importance.

In the United States, the first organized bench show was held in 1874 in conjunction with the meeting of the Illinois State Sportsmen's Association in Chicago, and all entries were dogs of sporting breeds. Although the show was a rather casual affair, interest spread quickly. Before the end of the year, shows were held in Oswego, New York, Mineola, Long Island, and Memphis, Tennessee. And the latter combined a bench show with the first organized field trial ever held in the United States. In January 1875, an all-breed show (the first in the United States) was held at Detroit, Michigan. From then on, interest increased rapidly, though rules were not always uniform, for there was no organization through which to coordinate activities until September 1884 when The American Kennel Club was founded. Now the largest dog registering organization in the world, the AKC is an association of several hundred member clubs—all breed, specialty, field trial, and obedience groups—each represented by a delegate to the AKC.

The several thousand shows and trials held annually in the United States do much to stimulate interest in breeding to produce better looking, sounder, purebred dogs. For breeders, shows provide a means of measuring the merits of their work as compared with accomplishments of other breeders. For hundreds of thousands of dog fanciers, they provide an absorbing hobby.

Bench Shows

At bench (or conformation) shows, dogs are rated comparatively on their physical qualities (or conformation) in accordance with breed Standards which have been approved by The American Kennel Club. Characteristics such as size, coat, color, placement of eye or ear, general soundness, etc., are the basis for selecting the best dog in a class. Only purebred dogs are eligible to compete and if the show is one where points toward a championship are to be awarded, a dog must be at least six months old.

Bench shows are of various types. An all-breed show has classes for all of the breeds recognized by The American Kennel Club as well as a Miscellaneous Class for breeds not recognized, such as the Australian Cattle Dog, the Ibizan Hound, the Spinoni Italiani, etc. A sanctioned match is an informal meeting where dogs compete but not for championship points. A specialty show is confined to a single breed. Other shows may restrict entries to champions of record, to American-bred dogs, etc. Competition for Junior Showmanship or for Best Brace, Best Team, or Best Local Dog may be included. Also, obedience competition is held in conjunction with many bench shows.

The term "bench show" is somewhat confusing in that shows of this type may be either "benched" or "unbenched." At the former, each dog is assigned an individual numbered stall where he must remain throughout the show except for times when he is being judged, groomed, or exercised. At unbenched shows, no stalls are provided and dogs are kept in their owners' cars or in crates when not being judged.

A show where a dog is judged for conformation actually constitutes an elimination contest. To begin with, the dogs of a single breed compete with others of their breed in one of the regular classes: Puppy, Novice, Bred by Exhibitor, American-Bred, or

Open, and, finally, Winners, where the top dogs of the preceding five classes meet. The next step is the judging for Best of Breed (or Best of Variety of Breed). Here the Winners Dog and Winners Bitch (or the dog named Winners if only one prize is awarded) compete with any champions that are entered, together with any undefeated dogs that have competed in additional non-regular classes. The dog named Best of Breed (or Best of Variety of Breed), then goes on to compete with the other Best of Breed winners in his Group. The dogs that win in Group competition then compete for the final and highest honor, Best in Show.

When the Winners Class is divided by sex, championship points are awarded the Winners Dog and Winners Bitch. If the Winners Class is not divided by sex, championship points are awarded the dog or bitch named Winners. The number of points awarded varies, depending upon such factors as the number of dogs competing, the Schedule of Points established by the Board of Directors of the AKC, and whether the dog goes on to win Best of Breed, the Group, and Best in Show.

In order to become a champion, a dog must win fifteen points, including points from at least two major wins—that is, at least two shows where three or more points are awarded. The major wins must be under two different judges, and one or more of the remaining points must be won under a third judge. The most points ever awarded at a show is five and the least is one, so, in order to become a champion, a dog must be exhibited and win in at least three shows, and usually he is shown many times before he wins his championship.

Pure Bred Dogs—American Kennel Gazette and other dog magazines contain lists of forthcoming shows, together with names and addresses of sponsoring organizations to which you may write for entry forms and information relative to fees, closing dates, etc. Before entering your dog in a show for the first time, you should familiarize yourself with the regulations and rules governing competition. You may secure such information from The American Kennel Club or from a local dog club specializing in your breed. It is essential that you also familiarize yourself with the AKC approved Standard for your breed so you will be fully aware of characteristics worthy of merit as well as those considered faulty, or possibly even serious enough to disqualify the dog from competition. For instance, monorchidism (failure of one testicle to descend) and cryptorchidism (failure of both testicles to descend) are disqualifying faults in all breeds.

If possible, you should first attend a show as a spectator and observe judging procedures from ringside. It will also be helpful to join a local breed club and to participate in sanctioned matches before entering an all-breed show.

The dog should be equipped with a narrow leather show lead and a show collar—never an ornamented or spiked collar. For benched shows, either a bench crate or a metal-link bench chain to fasten the dog to the bench will be needed. For unbenched shows, the dog's crate should be taken along so that he may be confined in comfort when he is not appearing in the ring. A dog should never be left in a car with all the windows closed. In hot weather the temperature will become unbearable in a very short time. Heat exhaustion may result from even a short period of confinement, and death may ensue.

Food and water dishes will be needed, as well as a supply of the food and water to which the dog is accustomed. Brushes and combs are also necessary, so that you may give the dog's coat a final grooming after you arrive at the show.

Familiarize yourself with the schedule of classes ahead of time, for the dog must be fed and exercised and permitted to relieve himself, and any last-minute grooming completed before his class is called. Both you and the dog should be ready to enter the ring unhurriedly. A good deal of skill in conditioning, training, and handling is required if a dog is to be presented properly. And it is essential that the handler himself be composed, for a jittery handler will transmit his nervousness to his dog.

Once the class is assembled in the ring, the judge will ask that the dogs be paraded in line, moving counter-clockwise in a circle. If you have trained your dog well, you will have no difficulty controlling him in the ring, where he must change pace quickly and gracefully and walk and trot elegantly and proudly with head erect. The show dog must also stand quietly for inspection, posing like a statue for several minutes while the judge observes his structure in detail, examines teeth, feet, coat, etc. When the judge calls your dog forward for individual inspection, do not attempt to converse, but answer any questions he may ask.

As the judge examines the class, he measures each dog against the ideal described in the Standard, then measures the dogs against each other in a comparative sense and selects for first place the dog that comes closest to conforming to the Standard for its breed. If your dog isn't among the winners, don't grumble. If he places first, don't brag loudly. For a bad loser is disgusting, but a poor winner is insufferable.

Junior Showmanship Competition at Westminster Kennel Club Show.

Bench crate.

Wagon crate.

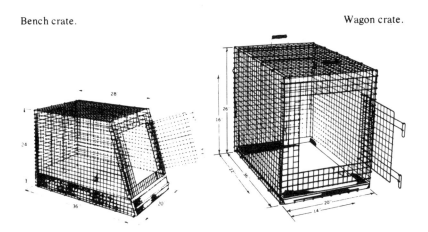

Collars. At the top are two "pinch" or "spiked" collars that are not permitted in AKC shows. Below are two permissible "choke" collars, the one on the right of steel chain and the one on the left of braided nylon. While the choke collars are permitted in conformation shows, they are used more often in obedience competition.

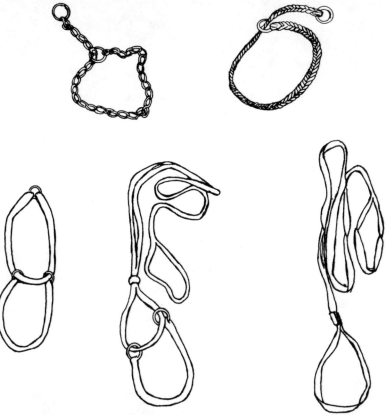

Left, "English" or "Martingale" collar to which lead would be attached. Center, "English" or "Martingale" collar and lead. In using either of these, the dog's head would be inserted through the lower loop. Right, nylon slip lead. Collars and leads of these three types are preferred for conformation showing because they give better control for stacking a dog than the "choke" collars.

Obedience Competition

For hundreds of years, dogs have been used in England and Germany in connection with police and guard work, and their working potential has been evaluated through tests devised to show agility, strength, and courage. Organized training has also been popular with English and German breeders for many years, although it was first practiced primarily for the purpose of training large breeds in aggressive tactics.

There was little interest in obedience training in the United States until 1933 when Mrs. Whitehouse Walker returned from England and enthusiastically introduced the sport. Two years later, Mrs. Walker persuaded The American Kennel Club to approve organized obedience activities and to assume jurisdiction over obedience rules. Since then, interest has increased at a phenomenal rate, for obedience competition is not only a sport the average spectator can follow readily, but also a sport for which the average owner can train his own dog easily. Obedience competition is suitable for all breeds. Furthermore, there is no limit to the number of dogs that may win in competition, for each dog is scored individually on the basis of a point rating system.

The dog is judged on his response to certain commands, and if he gains a high enough score in three successive trials under different judges, he wins an obedience degree. Degrees awarded are "CD"—Companion Dog; "CDX"—Companion Dog Excellent; and "UD"—Utility Dog. A fourth degree, the "TD" or Tracking Dog degree, may be won at any time and tests for it are held apart from dog shows. The qualifying score is a minimum of 170 points out of a possible total of 200, with no score in any one exercise less than 50% of the points allotted.

Since obedience titles are progressive, earlier titles (with the exception of the tracking degree) are dropped as a dog acquires the next higher degree. If an obedience title is gained in another country in addition to the United States, that fact is signified by the word "International," followed by the title.

Trials for obedience trained dogs are held at most of the larger bench shows, and obedience training clubs are to be found in almost all communities today. Information concerning forthcoming trials and lists of obedience training clubs are included regularly in *Pure Bred Dogs–American Kennel Gazette*—and other dog magazines. Pamphlets containing rules and regulations governing obedience competition are available upon request from The American Kennel Club, 51 Madison Avenue, New York, N.Y. 10010. Rules are revised occasionally, so if you are interested in participating in obedience competition, you should be sure your copy of the regulations is current.

All dogs must comply with the same rules, although in broad jump, high jump, and bar jump competition, the jumps are adjusted to the size of the breed. Classes at obedience trials are divided into Novice (A and B), Open (A and B), and Utility (which may be divided into A and B, at the option of the sponsoring club and with the approval of The American Kennel Club).

The Novice class is for dogs that have not won the title Companion Dog. In Novice A, no person who has previously handled a dog that has won a CD title in the obedience ring at a licensed or member trial, and no person who has regularly trained such a dog, may enter or handle a dog. The handler must be the dog's owner or a member of the owner's immediate family. In Novice B, dogs may be handled by the owner or any other person.

The Open A class is for dogs that have won the CD title but have not won the CDX title. Obedience judges and licensed handlers may not enter or handle dogs in this class. Each dog must be handled by the owner or by a member of his immediate family. The Open B class is for dogs that have won the title CD or CDX. A dog may continue to compete in this class after it has won the title UD. Dogs in this class may be handled by the owner or any other person.

The Utility class is for dogs that have won the title CDX. Dogs that have won the title UD may continue to compete in this class, and dogs may be handled by the owner or any other person. Provided the AKC approves, a club may choose to divide the Utility class into Utility A and Utility B. When this is done, the Utility A class is for dogs that have won the title CDX and have not won the title UD. Obedience judges and licensed handlers may not enter or handle dogs in this class. All other dogs that are eligible for the Utility class but not eligible for Utility A may be entered in Utility B.

Novice competition includes such exercises as heeling on and off lead, the stand for examination, coming on recall, and the long sit and the long down.

In Open competition, the dog must perform such exercises as heeling free, the drop on recall, and the retrieve on the flat and over the high jump. Also, he must execute the broad jump, and the long sit and long down.

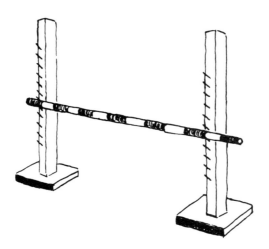

Bar Jump.

In the Utility class, competition includes scent discrimination, the directed retrieve, the signal exercise, directed jumping, and the group examination.

Tracking is the most difficult test. It is always done out-of-doors, of course, and, for obvious reasons, cannot be held at a dog show. The dog must follow a scent trail that is about a quarter mile in length. He is also required to find a scent object (glove, wallet, or other article) left by a stranger who has walked the course to lay down the scent. The dog is required to follow the trail a half to two hours after the scent is laid.

An ideal way to train a dog for obedience competition is to join an obedience class or a training club. In organized class work, beginners' classes cover pretty much the same exercises as those described in the chapter on manners. However, through class work you will develop greater precision than is possible in training your dog by yourself. Amateur handlers often cause the dog to be penalized, for if the handler fails to abide by the rules, it is the dog that suffers the penalty. A common infraction of the rules is using more than one signal or command where regulations stipulate only one may be used. Classwork will help eliminate such errors, which the owner may make unconsciously if he is working alone. Working with a class will also acquaint both dog and handler with ring procedure so that obedience trials will not present unforeseen problems.

Thirty or forty owners and dogs often comprise a class, and exercises are performed in unison, with individual instruction provided if it is required. The procedure followed in training—in fact, even wording of various commands—may vary from instructor to instructor. Equipment used will vary somewhat, also, but will usually include a training collar and leash, a long line, a dumbbell, and a jumping stick. The latter may be a short length of heavy doweling or a broom handle and both it and the dumbbell are usually painted white for increased visibility.

A bitch in season must never be taken to a training class, so before enrolling a female dog, you should determine whether she may be expected to come into season before classes are scheduled to end. If you think she will, it is better to wait and enroll her in a later course, rather than start the course and then miss classes for several weeks.

In addition to the time devoted to actual work in class, the dog must have regular, daily training sessions for practice at home. Before each class or home training session, the dog should be exercised so he will not be highly excited when the session starts, and he must be given an opportunity to relieve himself before the session begins. (Should he have an accident during the class, it is your responsibility to clean up after him.) The dog should be fed several hours before time for the class to begin or else after the class is over—never just before going to class.

If you decide to enter your dog in obedience competition, it is well to enter a small, informal show the first time. Dogs are usually called in the order in which their names appear in the catalog, so as soon as you arrive at the show, acquaint yourself with the schedule. If your dog is not the first to be judged, spend some time at ringside, observing the routine so you will know what to expect when your dog's turn comes.

In addition to collar, leash, and other equipment, you should take your dog's food and water pans and a supply of the food and water to which he is accustomed. You should also take his brushes and combs in order to give him a last-minute brushing before you enter the ring. It is important that the dog look his best even though he isn't to be judged on his appearance.

Before entering the ring, exercise your dog, give him a drink of water, and permit him to relieve himself. Once your dog enters the ring, give him your full attention and be sure to give voice commands distinctly so he will hear and understand, for there will be many distractions at ringside.

Dumbbells.

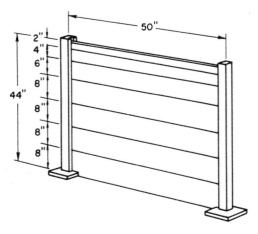

Solid hurdle.

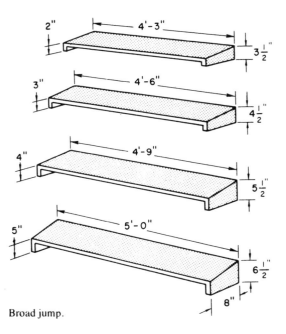

Broad jump.

Top dogs in Utility Class. This illustrates the variety of breeds that compete in obedience.

Genetics

Genetics, the science of heredity, deals with the processes by which physical and mental traits of parents are transmitted to offspring. For centuries, man has been trying to solve these puzzles, but only in the last two hundred years has significant progress been made.

During the eighteenth century, Kölreuter, a German scientist, made revolutionary discoveries concerning plant sexuality and hybridization but was unable to explain just how hereditary processes worked. In the middle of the nineteenth century, Gregor Johann Mendel, an Augustinian monk, experimented with the ordinary garden pea and made other discoveries of major significance. He found that an inherited characteristic was inherited as a complete unit, and that certain characteristics predominated over others. Next, he observed that the hereditary characteristics of each parent are contained in each offspring, even when they are not visible, and that "hidden" characteristics can be transferred without change in their nature to the grandchildren, or even later generations. Finally, he concluded that although heredity contains an element of uncertainty, some things are predictable on the basis of well-defined mathematical laws.

Unfortunately, Mendel's published paper went unheeded, and when he died in 1884 he was still virtually unknown to the scientific world. But other researchers were making discoveries, too. In 1900, three different scientists reported to learned societies that much of their research in hereditary principles had been proved years before by Gregor Mendel and that findings matched perfectly.

Thus, hereditary traits were proved to be transmitted through the chromosomes found in pairs in every living being, one of each pair contributed by the mother, the other by the father. Within each chromosome have been found hundreds of smaller structures, or genes, which are the actual determinants of hereditary characteristics. Some genes are dominant and will be seen in the offspring. Others are recessive and will not be outwardly apparent, yet can be passed on to the offspring to combine with a similar recessive gene of the other parent and thus be seen. Or they may be passed on to the offspring, not be outwardly apparent, but be passed on again to become apparent in a later generation.

Once the genetic theory of inheritance became widely known, scientists began drawing a well-defined line between inheritance and environment. More recent studies show some overlapping of these influences and indicate a combination of the two may be responsible for certain characteristics. For instance, studies have proved that extreme cold increases the amount of black pigment in the skin and hair of the "Himalayan" rabbit, although it has little or no effect on the white or colored rabbit. Current research also indicates that even though characteristics are determined by the genes, some environmental stress occurring at a particular period of pregnancy might cause physical change in the embryo.

Long before breeders had any knowledge of genetics, they practiced one of its most important principles—selective breeding. Experience quickly showed that "like begets like," and by breeding like with like and discarding unlike offspring, the various individual breeds were developed to the point where variations were relatively few. Selective breeding is based on the idea of maintaining the quality of a breed at the highest possible level, while improving whatever defects are prevalent. It requires that only the top dogs in a litter be kept for later breeding, and that inferior specimens be ruthlessly eliminated.

In planning any breeding program, the first requisite is a definite goal—that is, to have clearly in mind a definite picture of the type of dog you wish eventually to produce. To attempt to breed perfection is to approach the problem unrealistically. But if you don't breed for improvement, it is preferable that you not breed at all.

As a first step, you should select a bitch that exemplifies as many of the desired characteristics as possible and mate her with a dog that also has as many of the desired characteristics as possible. If you start with mediocre pets, you will produce mediocre pet puppies. If you decide to start with more than one bitch, all should closely approach the type you desire, since you will then stand a better chance of producing uniformly good puppies from all. Breeders often start with a single bitch and keep the best bitches in every succeeding generation.

Experienced breeders look for "prepotency" in breeding stock—that is, the ability of a dog or bitch to transmit traits to most or all of its offspring. While the term is usually used to describe the transmission of good qualities, a dog may also be prepotent in

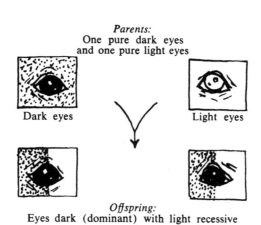

Parents:
One pure dark eyes
and one pure light eyes

Dark eyes   Light eyes

Offspring:
Eyes dark (dominant) with light recessive

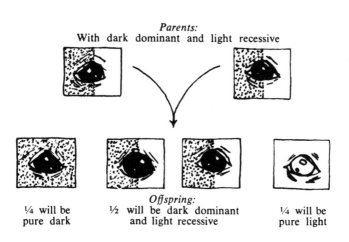

Parents:
With dark dominant and light recessive

¼ will be
pure dark

Offspring:
½ will be dark dominant
and light recessive

¼ will be
pure light

The above is a schematic representation of the Mendelian law as it applies to the inheritance of eye color. The law applies in the same way to the inheritance of other physical characteristics.

transmitting faults. To be prepotent in a practical sense, a dog must possess many characteristics controlled by dominant genes. If desired characteristics are recessive, they will be apparent in the offspring only if carried by both sire and dam. Prepotent dogs and bitches usually come from a line of prepotent ancestors, but the mere fact that a dog has exceptional ancestors will not necessarily mean that he himself will produce exceptional offspring.

A single dog may sire a tremendous number of puppies, whereas a bitch can produce only a comparatively few litters during her lifetime. Thus, a sire's influence may be very widespread as compared to that of a bitch. But in evaluating a particular litter, it must be remembered that the bitch has had as much influence as has had the dog.

Inbreeding, line-breeding, outcrossing, or a combination of the three are the methods commonly used in selective breeding.

Inbreeding is the mating together of closely related animals, such as father-daughter, mother-son, or brother-sister. Although some breeders insist such breeding will lead to the production of defective individuals, it is through rigid inbreeding that all breeds of dogs have been established. Controlled tests have shown that any harmful effects appear within the first five or ten generations, and that if rigid selection is exercised from the beginning, a vigorous inbred strain will be built up.

Line-breeding is also the mating together of individuals related by family lines. However, matings are made not so much on the basis of the dog's and bitch's relationship to each other, but, instead, on the basis of their relationship to a highly admired ancestor, with a view to perpetuating that ancestor's qualities. Line-breeding constitutes a long-range program and cannot be accomplished in a single generation.

Outcrossing is the breeding together of two dogs that are unrelated in family lines. Actually, since breeds have been developed through the mating of close relatives, all dogs within any given breed are related to some extent. There are few breedings that are true outcrosses, but if there is no common ancestor within five generations, a mating is usually considered an outcross.

Experienced breeders sometimes outcross for one generation in order to eliminate a particular fault, then go back to inbreeding or line-breeding. Neither the good effects nor the bad effects of outcrossing can be truly evaluated in a single mating, for undesirable recessive traits may be introduced into a strain, yet not show up for several generations. Outcrossing is better left to experienced breeders, for continual outcrossing results in a wide variation in type and great uncertainty as to the results that may be expected.

Two serious defects that are believed heritable—subluxation and orchidism—should be zealously guarded against, and afflicted dogs and their offspring should be eliminated from breeding programs. Subluxation is a condition of the hip joint where the bone of the socket is eroded and the head of the thigh bone is also worn away, causing lameness which becomes progressively more serious until the dog is unable to walk. Orchidism is the failure of one or both testicles to develop and descend properly. When one testicle is involved, the term "monorchid" is used. When both are involved, "cryptorchid" is used. A cryptorchid is almost always sterile, whereas a monorchid is usually fertile. There is evidence that orchidism "runs in families" and that a monorchid transmits the tendency through bitch and male puppies alike.

Through the years, many misconceptions concerning heredity have been perpetuated. Perhaps the one most widely perpetuated is the idea evolved hundreds of years ago that somehow characteristics were passed on through the mixing of the blood of the parents. We still use terminology evolved from that theory when we speak of bloodlines, or describe individuals as full-blooded, despite the fact that the theory was disproved more than a century ago.

Also inaccurate and misleading is any statement that a definite fraction or proportion of an animal's inherited characteristics can be positively attributed to a particular ancestor. Individuals lacking knowledge of genetics sometimes declare that an individual receives half his inherited characteristics from each parent, a quarter from each grandparent, an eighth from each great-grandparent, etc. Thousands of volumes of scientific findings have been published, but no simple way has been found to determine positively which characteristics have been inherited from which ancestors, for the science of heredity is infinitely complex.

Any breeder interested in starting a serious breeding program should study several of the books on canine genetics and breeding and whelping that are currently available. Two excellent works covering these subjects are *Meisen Breeding Manual,* by Hilda Meisenzahl, and *The Standard Book of Dog Breeding,* by Dr. Alvin Grossman—both published by the publisher of this book.

Whelping box. Detail at right shows proper side-wall construction which helps keep small puppies confined and provides sheltered nook to prevent crushing or smothering.

Breeding and Whelping

The breeding life of a bitch begins when she comes into season the first time at the age of eight to ten months. Thereafter, she will come in season at roughly six-month intervals. Her maximum fertility builds up from puberty to full maturity and then declines until a state of total sterility is reached in old age. Just when this occurs is hard to determine, for the fact that an older bitch shows signs of being in season doesn't necessarily mean she is still capable of reproducing.

The length of the season varies from eighteen to twenty-one days. The first indication is a pronounced swelling of the vulva with coincidental bleeding (called "showing color") for about the first seven to nine days. The discharge gradually turns to a creamy color, and it is during this phase (estrus), from about the tenth to the fifteenth days, that the bitch is ovulating and is receptive to the male. The ripe, unfertilized ova survive for about seventy-two hours. If fertilization doesn't occur, the ova die and are discharged the next time the bitch comes in season. If fertilization does take place, each ovum attaches itself to the walls of the uterus, a membrane forms to seal it off, and a foetus develops from it.

Following the estrus phase, the bitch is still in season until about the twenty-first day and will continue to be attractive to males, although she will usually fight them off as she did the first few days. Nevertheless, to avoid accidental mating, the bitch must be confined for the entire period. Virtual imprisonment is necessary, for male dogs display uncanny abilities in their efforts to reach a bitch in season.

The odor that attracts the males is present in the bitch's urine, so it is advisable to take her a good distance from the house before permitting her to relieve herself. To eliminate problems completely, your veterinarian can prescribe a preparation that will disguise the odor but will not interfere with breeding when the time is right. Many fanciers use such preparations when exhibiting a bitch and find that nearby males show no interest whatsoever. But it is not advisable to permit a bitch to run loose when she has been given a product of this type, for during estrus she will seek the company of male dogs and an accidental mating may occur.

A potential brood bitch, regardless of breed, should have good bone, ample breadth and depth of ribbing, and adequate room in the pelvic region. Unless a bitch is physically mature—well beyond the puppy stage when she has her first season—breeding should be delayed until her second or a later season. Furthermore, even though it is possible for a bitch to conceive twice a year, she should not be bred oftener than once a year. A bitch that is bred too often will age prematurely and her puppies are likely to lack vigor.

Two or three months before a bitch is to be mated, her physical condition should be considered carefully. If she is too thin, provide a rich, balanced diet plus the regular exercise needed to develop strong, supple muscles. Daily exercise on the lead is as necessary for the too-thin bitch as for the too-fat one, although the latter will need more exercise and at a brisker pace, as well as a reduction of food, if she is to be brought to optimum condition. A prospective brood bitch must have had permanent distemper shots as well as rabies vaccination. And a month before her season is due, a veterinarian should examine a stool specimen for worms. If there is evidence of infestation, the bitch should be wormed.

A dog may be used at stud from the time he reaches physical maturity, well on into old age. The first time your bitch is bred, it is well to use a stud that has already proven his ability by having sired other litters. The fact that a neighbor's dog is readily available should not influence your choice, for to produce the best puppies, you must select the stud most suitable from a genetic standpoint.

If the stud you prefer is not going to be available at the time your bitch is to be in season, you may wish to consult your veterinarian concerning medications available for inhibiting the onset of the season. With such preparations, the bitch's season can be delayed indefinitely.

Usually the first service will be successful. However, if it isn't, in most cases an additional service is given free, provided the stud dog is still in the possession of the same owner. If the bitch misses, it may be because her cycle varies widely from normal. Through microscopic examination, a veterinarian can determine exactly when the bitch is entering the estrus phase and thus is likely to conceive.

The owner of the stud should give you a stud-service certificate, providing a four-generation pedigree for the sire and showing the date of mating. The litter registration application is completed only after the puppies are whelped, but it, too, must be signed by the owner of the stud as well as the owner of the bitch. Registration forms may be secured by writing The American Kennel Club.

In normal pregnancy there is visible enlargement of the abdomen by the end of the fifth week. By palpation (feeling with the fingers) a veterinarian may be able to distinguish developing puppies as early as three weeks after mating, but it is unwise for a novice to poke and prod, and try to detect the presence of unborn puppies.

The gestation period normally lasts nine weeks, although it may vary from sixty-one to sixty-five days. If it goes beyond sixty-five days from the date of mating, a veterinarian should be consulted.

During the first four or five weeks, the bitch should be permitted her normal amount of activity. As she becomes heavier, she should be walked on the lead, but strenuous running and jumping should be avoided. Her diet should be well balanced (see page 41), and if she should become constipated, small amounts of mineral oil may be added to her food.

A whelping box should be secured about two weeks before the puppies are due, and the bitch should start then to use it as her bed so she will be accustomed to it by the time puppies arrive. Preferably, the box should be square, with each side long enough so that the bitch can stretch out full length and have several inches to spare at either end. The bottom should be padded with an old cotton rug or other material that is easily laundered. Edges of the padding should be tacked to the floor of the box so the puppies will not get caught in it and smother. Once it is obvious labor is about to begin, the padding should be covered with several layers of spread-out newspapers. Then, as papers become soiled, the top layer can be pulled off, leaving the area clean.

Forty-eight to seventy-two hours before the litter is to be whelped, a definite change in the shape of the abdomen will be noted. Instead of looking barrel-shaped, the abdomen will sag pendulously. Breasts usually redden and become enlarged, and milk may be present a day or two before the puppies are whelped. As the time becomes imminent, the bitch will probably scratch and root at her bedding in an effort to make a nest, and will refuse food and ask to be let out every few minutes. But the surest sign is a drop in temperature of two or three degrees about twelve hours before labor begins.

The bitch's abdomen and flanks will contract sharply when labor actually starts, and for a few minutes she will attempt to expel a puppy, then rest for a while and try again. Someone should stay with the bitch the entire time whelping is taking place, and if she appears to be having unusual difficulties, a veterinarian should be called.

Puppies are usually born head first, though some may be born feet first and no difficulty encountered. Each puppy is enclosed in a separate membranous sac that the bitch will remove with her teeth. She will sever the umbilical cord, which will be attached to the soft, spongy afterbirth that is expelled right after the puppy emerges. Usually the bitch eats the afterbirth, so it is necessary to watch and make sure one is expelled for each puppy whelped. If afterbirth is retained, the bitch may develop peritonitis and die.

The dam will lick and nuzzle each newborn puppy until it is warm and dry and ready to nurse. If puppies arrive so close together that she can't take care of them, you can help her by rubbing the puppies dry with a soft cloth. If several have been whelped but the bitch continues to be in labor, all but one should be removed and placed in a small box lined with clean towels and warmed to about seventy degrees. The bitch will be calmer if one puppy is left with her at all times.

Whelping sometimes continues as long as twenty-four hours for a very large litter, but a litter of two or three puppies may be whelped in an hour. When the bitch settles down, curls around the puppies and nuzzles them to her, it usually indicates that all have been whelped.

The bitch should be taken away for a few minutes while you clean the box and arrange clean padding. If her coat is soiled, sponge it clean before she returns to the puppies. Once she is back in the box, offer her a bowl of warm beef broth and a pan of cool water, placing both where she will not have to get up in order to reach them. As soon as she indicates interest in food, give her a generous bowl of chopped meat to which codliver oil and dicalcium phosphate have been added.

If inadequate amounts of calcium are provided during the period the puppies are nursing, eclampsia may develop. Symptoms are violent trembling, rapid rise in temperature, and rigidity of muscles. Veterinary assistance must be secured immediately, for death may result in a very short time. Treatment consists of massive doses of calcium gluconate administered intravenously, after which symptoms subside in a miraculously short time.

For weak or very small puppies, supplemental feeding is often recommended. Any one of three different methods may be used: tube-feeding (with a catheter attached to a syringe), using an eyedropper (this method requires great care in order to avoid getting formula in the lungs), or using a tiny bottle (the "pet nurser" available at most pet supply stores). The commercially prepared puppy formulas are most convenient and are readily obtainable from a veterinarian, who can also tell you which method of administering the formula is most practical in your particular case. It is important to remember that equipment must be kept scrupulously clean. It can be sterilized by boiling, or it may be soaked in a Clorox solution, then washed carefully and dried between feedings.

All puppies are born blind and their eyes open when they are ten to fourteen days old. At first the eyes have a bluish cast and appear weak, and the puppies must be protected from strong light until at least ten days after the eyes open.

To ensure proper emotional development, young dogs should be shielded from loud noises and rough handling. Being lifted by the front legs is painful and may result in permanent injury to the shoulders. So when lifting a puppy, always place one hand under the chest with the forefinger between the front legs, and place the other hand under his bottom.

Flannelized rubber sheeting is an ideal surface for the bottom of the bed for the new puppies. It is inexpensive and washable, and will provide a surface that will give the puppies traction so that they will not slip either while nursing or when learning to walk.

Sometimes the puppies' nails are so long and sharp that they scratch the bitch's breasts. Since the nails are soft, they can be trimmed with ordinary scissors.

At about four weeks of age, formula should be provided. The amount fed each day should be increased over a period of two weeks, when the puppies can be weaned completely. One of the commercially prepared formulas can be mixed according to directions on the container, or formula can be prepared at home in accordance with instructions from a veterinarian. The formula should be warmed to lukewarm, and poured into a shallow pan placed on the floor of the box. After his mouth has been dipped into the mixture a few times, a puppy will usually start to lap formula. All puppies should be allowed to eat from the same pan, but be sure the small ones get their share. If they are pushed aside, feed them separately. Permit the puppies to nurse part of the time, but gradually increase the number of meals of formula. By the time the puppies are five weeks old, the dam should be allowed with them only at night. When they are about six weeks old, they should be weaned completely. Three meals a day are usually sufficient from this time until the puppies are about three months old, when feedings are reduced to two a day. About the time the dog reaches one year of age, feedings may be reduced to one each day. (For further information on this subject, see page 38.)

Once they are weaned, puppies should be given temporary distemper injections every two weeks until they are old enough for permanent inoculations. At six weeks, stool specimens should be checked for worms, for almost without exception, puppies become infested. Specimens should be checked again at eight weeks, and as often thereafter as your veterinarian recommends.

Sometimes owners decide as a matter of convenience to have a bitch spayed or a male castrated. While this is recommended when a dog has a serious inheritable defect or when abnormalities of reproductive organs develop, in sound, normal purebred dogs, spaying a bitch or castrating a male may prove a definite disadvantage. The operations automatically bar dogs from competing in shows as well as precluding use for breeding. The operations are seldom dangerous, but they should not be performed without serious consideration of these facts.

Ch. Bo-Mar's Drummer Boy winning Miniature Pinscher Club of America Specialty.

Ch. Bo-Mar's Drum Call, Best of Opposite Sex at 1963 Miniature Pinscher Club of America Specialty.

Personality of
The Miniature Pinscher

The Miniature Pinscher, by virtue of its small size, adapts extremely well to urban or suburban living. As a matter of fact, we trained our first Miniature Pinscher to use "kitty litter" because we lived in a relatively small apartment in New England, and in the cold winter months neither she nor we cared to go for a walk in the snow.

The Pinscher is intelligent and easily trained. He has a tendency to be clean in all respects, and the shedding of the short coat constitutes minimal, if any, problems to the apartment dweller. On the other hand, the Miniature Pinscher certainly is not out of his element on the farm and has been trained to tree squirrels, chase rabbits, and even help herd cows. It is not unusual for the Miniature Pinscher on a farm to catch a rabbit that is equal to or larger than the size of the dog.

Our pups are allowed to run in two paddocks. One is approximately an acre in size, and the other about two acres. Although we now live in the southern climate where snakes are by no means uncommon during the summer months, our Min-Pins have kept the entire area completely devoid of snakes and rodents of all types. As a matter of fact, although we encourage wildlife in all forms by placing feeders in appropriate places, birds do not find it safe to settle down in one of the Min-Pin paddocks for feeding. The Miniature Pinscher is very swift and can stalk its prey with the best of hunters. Several of our Miniature Pinschers have actually caught birds and one of our more optimistic bitches, Ch. Bo-Mar's Drum Call, can frequently be seen chasing wildly across the paddock looking into the sky as if she had lost her mind. However, if you look carefully enough you will see a plane or a jet stream moving in the direction in which she is running. Having bagged a few birds, she still has great hopes of pulling in a Piper Cub.

The Miniature Pinscher attaches itself very quickly to children and really delights in joining a youngster in bed. As soon as the Min-Pin climbs onto the bed, he usually slips under the covers

131

like a mole, all the way to the foot of the bed. I have had the rather disquieting experience on several occasions of patting a small lump near the foot of the bed to smooth out the covers, only to feel the lump move and then to have a disgruntled Miniature Pinscher head appear from the covers.

For the apartment dweller, the puppy can be trained rather easily by being confined to a box, approximately three feet by four feet in size. Screen wire around a baby playpen makes a rather ideal situation for the Miniature Pinscher to be confined in when the owner does not desire the dog to have complete access to the house or apartment. Allowing the dog to go outside two or three times each day (after meals, etc.) will then give the small Miniature Pinscher adequate exercise. Furthermore, the dog will develop a fondness for the area in which he is kept and will not mind the confinement at all.

When we purchased our first Miniature Pinscher, we were quite concerned that she would be cold in the evenings, since she had been shipped to New England from the Deep South. Furthermore, our apartment, being just about everything that one could expect on a resident's salary, was not noted for its insulation or comfort. We, therefore, placed a small crate inside a baby playpen, and our pup slept there. We carefully wrapped a hot water bottle in rubberized flannel and placed it in the crate, and after a short period of time, the puppy began to associate the preparation of the hot water bottle with bedtime and would run to her crate as soon as she saw us prepare the hot water bottle. Shortly after she was six months of age, we sent the puppy out with Jane Kamp to participate in a show. Since this was our first experience with dog shows and handlers, we felt that it was quite important to tell the handler all our pup's peculiarities, and when we delivered her to the handler's kennel to start the show circuit, we took along the crate and hot water bottle and explained that "Gingerbread" (later to become Ch. Rebel-Roc's Cora von Kurt) would not go to bed without her hot water bottle. Our handler took it along with a slight grin. However, when she returned from the circuit she said, "By golly, you were right." She apparently took the young pup to the hotel room with her at night and found very quickly that the youngster raised "holy ned" until she got her hot water bottle.

"Ginger" was the delight of many New England fanciers because of her personality and showmanship, and she gave many people quite a chuckle when they came by the Min-Pin bench at the show and saw her straddling a hot water bottle to keep her "tummy" warm. She would leave the bottle long enough to go to the door of the benching crate to give the visitor an affectionate lick but then quickly returned to her comfortable "security bottle."

A friendly carpenter in Boston helped me prepare a rather elaborate whelping pen in our apartment, and our bitch stayed in it pretty well until the night that she decided to have the pups. She then insisted on getting into our bed, where, fortunately with the aid of a few large beach towels, we were able to accomplish the delivery without too much difficulty. After the three pups were born, the bitch was perfectly happy to be placed in the whelping pen with her new family and stayed there throughout the nursing period without objection.

The Min-Pin is a great tease, but, basically, he gets along well with any other dogs. We had the rather unique experience of having two Boxers and a Min-Pin bitch with three young pups in the same apartment and had minimal difficulty with this arrangement. It was rather amusing, however, to see the Miniature Pinscher steal bones from the Boxers. She would approach slowly, looking them clearly in the eye at all times, and then when she was in good shooting distance, she would paw the floor a little bit or make some other movement to distract the Boxer momentarily, and if she saw the jaws relax around the bone, she would grab the bone with the speed of lightning, and, having extracted it from the iron jaws of the Boxer, be well on her way to the next room before the Boxer realized what had occurred. Then the chase would begin.

The Min-Pin also had great fun with our baby daughter, and the two delighted in teasing each other. The six-month-old youngster would jump up and down in her "jump chair" and the Min-Pin would bark a couple of times and go scurrying around the chair at the speed of a motorcycle and then stop and wait until the child jumped again, when she would repeat the same wild circling about the chair. Frequently the two would transfer their action to the bed, where the six-month-old child, sitting in the middle of the bed, would slap the bed covers, and the Min-Pin would go circling

Ch. Rebel Roc's Starboarder, Best of Breed, Miniature Pinscher Club of America Specialty, June 21, 1967.

Ch. Ric Lor's Just Mimi, Marylan Specialty Show Winner. Breeder-ow er-handler, Claire Panichi.

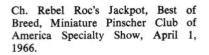

Ch. Rebel Roc's Jackpot, Best of Breed, Miniature Pinscher Club of America Specialty Show, April 1, 1966.

around her on the bed. They learned mutual respect for each other, and, although the Miniature Pinscher would grab the hand of the baby when the baby slapped her or pinched her, she would only squeeze hard enough to pay the youngster back for the offense, and never would she scratch the skin.

In spite of having as many as fifty Miniature Pinschers on our grounds and allowing the two youngsters complete access to every part of the kennel, neither child has ever been bitten by one of the Pinschers.

There is a six-year interval between our two children, and we were quite interested to see what the older Miniature Pinschers would do when the young son came along. As soon as he was old enough to toddle, he would go into the paddocks with us, and we were very amused to see the old patriarch of the kennel, Ch. Bo-Mar's Pepper Pot von Enztal, who had never been around small children at all, place himself across the lap of the baby and deny any of the other Pinschers the opportunity to approach and inspect this "new and strange animal."

The Miniature Pinscher is a very alert, adaptable animal. Temperament is basically good in this breed. Many people, referring to the Miniature Pinscher as a Miniature Doberman (which, of course, is erroneous), ask whether or not the Miniature Pinscher possesses the "sharp" temperament that is said to be characteristic of the Doberman Pinscher. It is, of course, difficult to generalize. However, I believe it is quite safe to say that the Miniature Pinscher, although alert and aggressive, is not vicious. He adjusts very well to people of all ages, and he may indeed become quite possessive of his owner or owners. On the other hand, if properly trained, he will be quite willing to accept newcomers with ease. In developing proper temperament, environment, obviously, is just as important as genetics, if not more so.

Our original Miniature Pinscher, who lived very closely with us in an apartment during my residency training days, is still the world's best salesman for the breed. As a matter of fact, she even shows *preference* for someone she has not met before, and as soon as a stranger has a seat in our recreation room, she very quickly asks his permission to sit on his lap and, preferably, to be allowed to give his chin a lick or two. She becomes especially attached to the women who have nice smelling lotion on their hands and will lick their hands as long as allowed. She gives a quick bark when someone comes to the door, but it is not a bark of anger or fear. It is more a bark to tell the family to come along and greet the visitor. When new folks come into the foyer, she literally greets them with a smiling face and a little wiggle of her rear. The average Miniature Pinscher is probably not quite so gregarious and, in general, will tend to be slightly reserved, yet friendly.

The hearing of the Miniature Pinscher is extremely acute, and it is particularly interesting to watch the Pinscher respond to the approach of a visitor long before a member of one of the larger breeds gives any evidence of hearing a sound. The acuteness of the Min-Pin's hearing reminds me of the anecdote in which a shopkeeper sold a Great Dane as a watch dog to an individual who was having trouble with burglars. After the Dane had slept through a burglary or so, the buyer went back to the shop to complain, and instead of offering a refund, the pet shop owner said, "What you need is a little dog to wake the big dog up." Certainly, the Miniature Pinscher would fill the bill in this instance because he is an excellent watch dog. Where another animal in concerned, the Miniature Pinscher has no fear. It is not at all unusual to see a Miniature Pinscher stand off a Dane or German Shepherd at a show. Min-Pins certainly have the heart of a lion and live up to their reputation of being a big dog in a little package, and, in all respects, "The King of the Toys."

From the breeding standpoint the Miniature Pinscher owner is in a very fortunate position. The Min-Pin mothers are usually very good whelpers, and in spite of the fact that we have been breeding rather consistently for about ten years, we have yet to have our first Caesarean section. Furthermore, the dams are usually very adequate in caring for the young, and, in general, have a good supply of milk. It is quite unusual to have to supplement the feeding of the puppies of the new Miniature Pinscher litter.

The Min-Pin is an excellent performer when it comes to bench shows, and adapts unusually well to obedience training, also. Obedience training in the Min-Pin, just as in any other breed, makes the animal a much more desirable house pet, but it is not unusual

136

for a member of the breed to excel in obedience competition to such an extent as to appear as the highest scoring dog in a trial. And several Miniature Pinschers have done quite well both in conformation and obedience.

Among Miniature Pinscher fanciers who have engaged in obedience are Miss Ann Dutton and Camille Robertson of the Sanbrook Kennels, Mrs. Barbara Finley of the Bar-Pin Kennels, and Mrs. Catherine J. Marshall of Spokane, Washington. Mrs. Marshall owns Wee Midget von Blitzen, C. D. X., Canadian C. D., who was highest scoring dog at Lewiston, Idaho, in 1961 with a score of 200, and at Missoula, Montana, in June of 1961, with a score of 198.5 Unfortunately, Midget had to retire before receiving her U. D. degree because of a leg injury. Other obedience trained Min-Pins owned by Mrs. Marshall are Urray Golden Penny, II, C. D. X., Canadian C. D., the highest scoring dog in many events, and Kapenni Kupfer Kricket, C. D. X., Canadian C. D. Kricket was highest scoring dog—with a score of 198.5—at the Electric Kennel Club Show at Great Falls, Montana, in June of 1966, when she was just seven months of age.

"Tom-Tom" and Patty Boshell with Dr. Boshell and Ch. Rebel Roc's Starboarder, Best in Show in Louisville, Kentucky, 1967.

Ch. Bo-Mar's Drum Son, first Sweepstakes Winner. Owners, J. R. McNamara and Dr. B. R. Boshell.

Ch. Bo-Mar's Drummer Boy and Ch. Bo-Mar's Drum Call, Best of Opposite Sex and Best of Breed at St. Petersburg, Florida, Show, June 11, 1967.

Ch. Halrok Hi Lili, Winners Bitch at 1966 Westminster Kennel Club Show. Bred by Vera Halpin and co-owned by Vera Halpin and Judy Moser. Judge, E. L. Pickhardt.

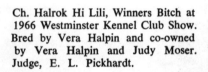

Miniature Pinscher Clubs

The primary purpose of any dog breed club is to bring together breeders and fanciers who share common interests and are willing to pool their knowledge and work together to promote the betterment of the breed. The new owner of a Miniature Pinscher—whether his dog is a puppy or an adult—will do well to consider becoming a member of a Miniature Pinscher club if he has any aspirations toward participation in bench shows, obedience training programs, or future breeding operations. In fact, whether he has any such aspirations or not, any owner of a Min-Pin will find membership in a club a rewarding and enriching experience.

The Miniature Pinscher Club of America was formed in 1929 and recognized by The American Kennel Club shortly thereafter. The Standard for the breed was approved by The American Kennel Club in 1935 and subsequently revised in February 1950. Initially, the Miniature Pinscher was shown in the Terrier Group, but subsequently it was placed in the Toy Group of dogs, where it has remained. One of the early problems was breeding an animal that would fit the Standard and still be within the size limit prescribed for the breed—i. e., ten to twelve and a half inches. That problem has been pretty well solved by the serious Miniature Pinscher breeders who practice selective breeding, and today's good sound show specimen conforms to the Standard very well indeed, while he remains well within the limitation for size.

The Miniature Pinscher was immediately quite popular but has never risen to the position in the public eye that the Cocker, Chihuahua, Boxer, and Poodle have enjoyed. In spite of this, however, the Miniature Pinscher has been able to carry his weight quite nicely in the Toy Groups and has also won a reasonable number of Best-in-Show awards. The first Group won by a Miniature Pinscher apparently was in Chicago in 1935. Much of the success of the Miniature Pinscher in the show ring can be attributed to the work of the members of the Miniature Pinscher Club of America, both individually and as a group.

The members of the Miniature Pinscher Club of America are

widely distributed over the country, but in addition to the parent club, regional clubs have been formed in California, Texas, Maryland, the New York-New England area, and in the Midwest. Prospective members will find names and addresses of secretaries of both the parent and regional clubs listed in the various dog publications on sale at pet shops and newsstands, or available in the reference sections of public libraries.

The Midwestern Miniature Pinscher Club was organized in November 1966 at the Grand Rapids, Michigan, Show. The first president was Clinton R. Craig; vice president, John McNamara; secretary, Carol Hoffman; and treasurer, Bertha McAllister. By the end of the first year of its existence, the club's membership had grown to forty-five.

The Eastern Miniature Pinscher Club organizers had their charter meeting on September 1, 1963. Since that time they have met quarterly and have published a quarterly "News-Letter" which is mailed out regularly to all devotees of the breed. Each year a specialty show is held in conjunction with the Trenton All-Breed Show. Following the specialty, the club sponsors a buffet dinner. In addition to the specialty show, a regular fun match and picnic are held each year and a special reunion is held in conjunction with the Westminster Show in February each year.

The first Eastern Miniature Pinscher Specialty Show was held in 1964 with an entry of forty-two dogs. The Show was judged by Miss Anna Katherine Nicholas and was won by Bo-Mar's Drummer Boy, who at that time was eight months of age and came from the Classes to make the win. Ch. Bo-Mar's Ginger Snap was Best of Opposite Sex.

In 1965 the show was judged by Mr. E. W. Tipton, Jr., and there was an entry of fifty-two dogs. This show was won by Ch. Bel-Roc's Buster Brown, owned by Mrs. F. P. Booher, and Ch. Bo-Mar's Drum Call was Best of Opposite Sex.

The 1966 specialty was judged by Dr. Buris R. Boshell and the entry was fifty-four on this occasion. Best-of-Breed winner was Ch. Del Crest's Dona Mite, owned by Mrs. Della Harris.

Mrs. Yan Paul was on the "Wool Sack" for the 1967 event. She drew an entry of fifty-three dogs, and the Best of Breed was again won by Ch. Bo-Mar's Drummer Boy, owned by Dr. Buris R. Boshell.

The first meeting of the Dallas Miniature Pinscher Club was

held May 28, 1956. No name was selected for the Club at that time, and only one officer was elected—Miss Ann Thurman, who served as secretary.

After holding two required Plan A Matches and one extra Plan B Match, the club was licensed for shows by The American Kennel Club and the first one was held March 20, 1959. There were twenty-six entries and twenty-five dogs at the first show, with Col. M. J. Grace of Dallas as judge. Ch. Martin's Symbols of the Hill won Best in Show with L. E. Piper handling. Mrs. James D. Ringo of Pine Bluff, Arkansas, was the owner.

In 1960 an entry of twenty-seven dogs was judged by Mr. Paul Berlowitz, who named Ch. Roy Bee's Marck v. Akers as Best in Show. Mr. Pete Paterson was the handler and Mr. and Mrs. David H. Akers of Dallas were owners of the winning dog.

1961 brought an entry of twenty-five dogs judged by Col. M. J. Grace. Best in Show was won by Ch. King's Hi Fashion Image of Mira, a young bitch owned by Dr. and Mrs. C. D. Bourke, Jr., of Fort Worth.

In 1962 the entry of twenty-two dogs was judged by Rex L. Vanderventer. Best in Show was Ch. Rebel Roc's Casanova von Kurt, a young dog owned by Mrs. E. W. Tipton, Kingsport, Tennessee.

1963's entry was forty dogs. Porter Washington was on the "Wool Sack," and Best in Show was Ch. Camille von Glick, a young bitch handled by Larry Downey and owned by Marie C. Schneider, Glenview, Illinois.

1964 produced thirty-seven entries judged by Chris. Shuttleworth. Best in Show was Ch. King's High Fashion Copper, owned by W. A. King of Fort Worth.

An entry of twenty-seven dogs in 1965 was judged by E. W. Tipton, Jr. Best in Show was Ch. Bo-Mar's Drum Call, a young bitch owned by Mrs. Mary Alice Sticklin, Centralia, Washington.

L. E. Piper judged the 1966 show with an entry of twenty-two dogs. Best in Show was Ch. Bo-Mar's Drummer Boy, a young dog handled by Clara Alford and owned by Dr. Buris R. Boshell.

The 1967 show brought Dr. Buris R. Boshell to the "Wool Sack" with an entry of thirty-nine dogs. Best in Show was Ch. Haldee von Glick, owned by Avis B. Flynn of Dallas. Clara Alford judged the November 1967 specialty, selecting the Maynard Helm's Gunner General for the Best-of-Breed spot.

141

Ch. Chaman Beeswing, owned by Lionel Hamilton Renwick, England.

Ch. Birling Painted Lady, bred by Lionel Hamilton Renwick, England.

Ch. Birling Wawocan Constellation, bred by Lionel Hamilton Renwick, England.

Ch. Birling Starlight, bred by Lionel Hamilton Renwick, England.

Min-Pins in Great Britain

By John Stott

As chairman of the English Min-Pin Club and the first Honorary Member of the M. P. C. A., I am delighted to contribute this chapter. No English kennels will be named; we live in a small country, and an omission or over-praise can hurt very much.

The Min-Pin was practically unknown here until one or two imports in the 1950-55 period attracted attention. By 1960 the vogue had set in, and imports had been made from Holland, Belgium, Austria, and the U. S. A. Each importing kennel seemed to produce stock of different types according to the country of origin. Today it is still possible to see the type of these early imports in spite of much interbreeding since those early days. Breeders can be heard to refer to the "U. S. A." or the "Continental" type.

The "U. S. A." type is generally very elegant with a good reach of neck and a clean Hackney action; the "Continental" type is a sound and sturdy specimen with perhaps a shorter foreface and less reach of neck. It is not for me to express any preference for either type, but in looking at the pedigrees of the Best of Breed, Best Puppy Dog, and Best Puppy Bitch, at Cruft's Show in London in 1967, I noted that each of these three had on the male side of its breeding a very potent sire, Ch. Culandhu Para Handy, whose male line was only three generations removed from U. S. A. dogs of von Enztal, Baum's, and Reedlynde breeding, with some admixture of Dutch blood from an early import from Holland.

Many of the early importers and breeders left the breed after a few years when the initial vogue had settled down and the breed had become one of the "middle level" Toy breeds, with registrations of about 250 a year and thirteen championship shows at which the necessary challenge certificates, three of which are required to qualify a champion, can be won. It is important to realize that here, to win one of these coveted challenge certificates, a dog has to meet all comers, perhaps even three or four established champions. A young champion can block the way of all other aspirants for several years if he is shown hard. This can be very frustrating, but it does generally mean that type has to improve over the years to outclass one of the "big boys." This is a challenge to the smaller breeder, and one of the reasons why we do not adopt the "points" system of qualification for champions.

In my several visits to the U. S. A., I never saw a blue or chocolate Min-Pin on exhibition. From our European imports we occasionally produce these, and in 1967 one quite elegant blue was placed at several of our championship shows. One paradox of our breed Standard is that dark pigmentation is mandatory, but in Europe, blues or chocolates can have off-black pigmentation. Even today, ten years after the early imports from Europe, we find occasional red noses and pale nails from breeding from European stock. This makes judging a little difficult at times!

Here, ears are not cropped or cut in any way. Most of the early exhibits were drop-eared, but now the majority have good small erect ears obtained by selective breeding; some kennels now can guarantee erect ears in nearly every litter. There is no doubt in my mind that erect ears improve the breed very much, and in Britain we see no reason why, in a humane country like the U. S. A., with a far greater Min-Pin population, cutting of the ears cannot be abandoned with great advantage to the beauty of the breed. Imports from the U. S. A. or from Europe have been used here to produce erect ears in a few generations, and there is no reason why this should not be done elsewhere from the same foundation stock.

At shows in the U. S. A. I have been impressed always by the deadly serious nature of the competition and by the tremendous effort that has gone into the training and handling of the exhibits. Ring deportment is at a much higher standard than with us, with one or two exceptions. The Min-Pin here that has been trained to a U. S. A. standard of showmanship and deportment always wins in Groups or Varieties, particularly at our huge Open Shows in the summer, where perhaps 2,000 dogs fight it out. The year 1967 saw Min-Pins winning Best Puppy or Best Toy, and even Best in Show against all comers, to a degree that has delighted all lovers of the breed.

Problems we have in plenty. Our black and tans are losing the dark rich tan which was so typical and so attractive, and most judges now accept a very inferior light tan. The proper Hackney action, so typical of our breed, is at a discount. One or two of our most experienced judges always walk to the side of the ring to see a Min-Pin pass them to check its action, but they are in the minority. The specimens with the true action are generally found to be predominantly bred from U. S. A. imports; the finest specimen of this true action was a great dog, Ch. Chaman Pawnee, bred in Scotland, whose action I have never seen bettered, but unfortunately he was lost when young in a kennel fire. He did leave a son, Ch. Para Handy, referred to earlier, who sired many of our most elegant winners. The great problem of defective rear action due to patellar subluxation has been almost entirely eliminated by selective breeding and rejection of unsound specimens, but this has required great patience on the part of the exhibitors, because this defect often arose in the fine-boned and elegant type so liked by the judges. Perhaps we have been helped in our approach to this problem by the presence in our circle of exhibitors of several experienced veterinary surgeons and medical doctors, who have been quick to recognize these defects.

The Miniature Pinscher Club in Britain is a small but intimate circle, whose members see each other regularly at least a dozen times a year. We have been fortunate in having a Club Show (your Specialty) for several years. This is a most friendly affair held in the middle of the country in the fall and producing an entry of about sixty dogs for one of our breeder-judges to run the rule over. The contrast between the ornate surroundings of Chicago and our own Burton on Trent Town Hall is very great, but the best beer in the world is brewed there, so a good time is generally had by all. Any visitor from another country who wishes to see the best of our stock could not do better than visit our Club show. Details of this event and all other Club activities can be obtained from the Honorary Secretary.

There is often argument in Britain as to the original make-up of the Min-Pin. It is generally accepted that the Dachshund and the Italian Greyhound have played a major part. Newly born puppies look very like Dachshund puppies; the coloring is also suggestive of that breed. The Hackney action and occasional production of erect ears suggest that the Italian Greyhound was also used, as does the characteristic way in which a Min-Pin will cross its front legs when sitting at ease on a chair or bench. Whatever its origin, the Min-Pin has come to stay in Britain as a smart show dog and a good house pet.

Gesa v. Haingraben at ten months. Owner, Mrs. A. Rätz, Sweden.

Left, Swedish and Norwegian Ch. Tjustorps Troll. Right, Swedish and Danish Ch. Bobo v. d. Trouwe Vriendjes. Owner, Mrs. A. Rätz, Sweden.

The Min-Pin in Sweden

By Mrs. Agneta Ratz

Since 1905 Miniature Pinschers have appeared in Swedish dog shows. The earliest breeders imported dogs from Germany. The breakthrough came in 1915, when a few rough-haired dogs were imported. They took part in shows until 1927, but since then the variant has not been seen in the Swedish shows.

The Affenpinscher was also rare. Some were to be seen between 1920 and 1930, but they remain rare to this day, and only one was registered in 1967.

The smooth-haired Pinscher, however, has been on the increase. Beginning in 1920, more and more people became interested in this variety. Some of the early breeders of outstanding Min-Pins were: Kennel Assartorp, owned by Mrs. Ellen Lindeblad, who was the breeder of the first Miniature Pinschers to acquire Swedish championships; Kennel av Oscaria, owned by Mr. O. N. Holmstrom; Kennel Skarpoborg, owned by Mrs. Ellen Weslien; and Kennel Lilltorpet, owned by Mrs. H. Gerhard. Kennel Lilltorpet was taken over in 1957 by Mrs. Gerhard's daughter and her husband, Mr. O. Rodin, who are not active at the present time, having only a few show dogs left.

About 1930, Mrs. Olga Edqvist and Mrs. Ebba Moller (Kennel Tjustorp) became interested in Miniature Pinschers. Mrs. Moller remained interested in the breed for approximately thirty years and many successful dogs came from her kennel. In the beginning Mrs. Moller acquired breeding stock from the Kennel Ajas in Denmark and then continued to import from the Netherlands and Germany. Ch. Jopi v. d. Trouwe Vriendjes, Aidas Dietrich, and Ch. Aidas Fivianta were three Dutch dogs that were outstanding show winners. Another remarkable dog during the period from 1955 to 1962 was the German import, Axel von Nordhang, who was an international and Scandinavian champion. Axel was never beaten in the show ring and sired many good puppies.

In the 1930's Miniature Pinscher activity was lively. Breeders who became interested in the Min-Pin during this time included Mrs. Agnes Karlsson of the Tolereds Kennel, Mr. Gunnar Christersson of the Kennel Acostis, and Mrs. Sandra Larsson of the Kennel Auricco. During this period most of the Swedish breeding activities were based on Danish imports from the Ajas Kennels. During the 1940's, however, interest in German bloodlines was renewed and breeding stock from the German Kennels of Gretelheim and Siegerland—both with and without Danish blood—was widely used in Sweden.

Mr. Oskar Svensson of Kennel Bernstorp was very much interested in breeding stock from the Danish Kennel Ajas. Later he imported the Dutch Ch. Edelroth v. d. Trouwe Vriendjes—in his time the most successful dog in the show ring and as a sire.

Mrs. S. Littorin, a Swedish judge, wrote the following in "The Dogbook, 1957": "Swedish breeders have, during different times, turned to various countries to complete their breeding and in the latter years the Dutch dogs have been remarkable. The Dutch imports have, as a rule, taken the highest prices. They are sound, perhaps a little more steady than their forbearers with a real nose part and correct eyes. The legs are good both front and back."

Today, some fifteen years later, it is still the Dutch dogs that are exceptional, especially those from the Kennel Trouwe Vriendjes, and it is the offspring of Trouwe Vriendjes stock that win the top prizes in the shows.

Ch. Chrijstel V. D. Trouwe Vriendjes is still the unbeaten champion. International and Scandinavian Ch. Saroya, who comes from the Trouwe Vriendjes line, was unbeaten during 1966-1967 in the International Shows in Sweden, Denmark, and Norway. And Swedish and Danish Ch. Arko, at one year of age, acquired the championship titles.

There are no large Miniature Pinscher kennels in Sweden. Most of the successful breeders have about twenty breeding dogs and use their own dogs to breed the approximately 400 Miniature Pinscher puppies that are registered every year by the Swedish Kennel Club. In addition to the puppies registered with the Club, many more are born and sold without being registered, however.

The usual colors are black and tan and various shades of reds, but on November 17, 1966, a gray dog with yellow markings was whelped, and on March 18, 1968, a gray bitch was whelped—both puppies came from a black, Tjustorps Troll. The gray with yellow combination is very uncommon in Scandinavia. In fact, these two are the only ones known to exist here.

In November 1966 a new Pinscher variant was introduced into Sweden when Mrs. Agneta Ratz imported two Middle Pinscher puppies from Germany—Jana v. d. Birkenheide and Gesa v. Haingraben (Swedish and Danish champion). Then in 1967 Mrs. Ratz imported the dog, Bundes o Klubsieger Dago v. Engelsbach. In Sweden the Middle Pinscher is considered a very elegant dog of middle size (40-48 centimeters). He is a dashing, attentive, faithful, devoted dog, quick to learn, not unnecessarily noisy, but a perfect guard.

The most famous Min-Pin breeders in Sweden today are: Mrs. Agneta Ratz; Mrs. Vera Hedblom of Hedebos Kennel; Mr. and Mrs. O. Rodin of Kennel Lilltorpet; Mrs. Vivi-Anne Kyrk of Kykdalens Kennel; and Mrs. Ruth Bergman of Hunnebos Kennel.

Ch. Birling Bright Star, Top Min-Pin, 1967.

Birling Starturn, biggest winner in number of prizes in 1967.

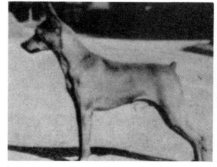

A note of appreciation to Miss Lee Tamboer, Mr. and Mrs. Paul Smith, and Mr. Lionel H. Renwick for the pictures of the unnamed, old-time Min-Pin painting, drawings, and sculptures.

The Miniature Pinscher
In Australia

By Mr. George Tucker

One sunny day in February 1958, an English freighter nosed her way through Sydney Heads, following much the same path as Captain Cook's "Endeavour" had pioneered a century and seventy years before. On board the freighter in a special hardwood shipping crate were two trail blazers of a different kind, whose seed of life had been sown in the United States, whose maturity must be credited to England, and whose fruits of a former and future union were destined to form the foundation of a different type of colony in Australia. So it was that the first Miniature Pinschers arrived "down under"—a gentleman who rejoiced in the name "Brazen of Tavey" and a young lady christened "Kanoon of Tavey," better known as "Tiny" and "Poppett" to their friends.

The male was whelped August 15th, 1954, imported in dam from the U. S. A. by Mr. and Mrs. F. Curnow of English Doberman fame. He was four times Best of Breed in England, including 1956-57 Cruft's Best in Show at the Southern County's Dog Show, England, and winner of the Miniature Pinscher's Club Daleviz Trophy. During his career in Australia he was Best in Show at the "4 P's All-Toy-Breeds Club's" Show in April 1958. His pedigree contained eight American champions. The female was whelped in quarantine in England, May 18, 1957, and was also imported in dam from U. S. A. She was not shown in England but her pedigree contained one international and eight American champions. Her litter brother was the winning dog at Cruft's in 1958. She was mated to a black and tan American Min-Pin before she left England and two bitch puppies were born in quarantine in Sydney. To Mr. George Byron of Sydney belongs the credit of purchasing this foundation stock. Puppies later bred by him were named under the Tasso prefix.

The mating of Kanoon of Tavey in England to the imported U. S. dog Delegate of Geddesburg produced Tasso Gypsy, who figured prominently in early Australian pedigrees. The way of a pathfinder in a breed is rarely strewn with roses and after a few litters Mr. Byron ceased breeding in 1960 for personal reasons and because of the difficulty in selling puppies of an unknown breed. This is where the story might have ended but for a stroke of good fortune, as it had attracted the attentions of at least one great admirer in Mrs. Margaret Spira of North Turramurra, Sydney, who had purchased two puppies from Mr. Byron and enthusiastically set about establishing the breed in Australia, founding the Pindom prefix. Prominent and popular in the Australian dog world, and highly regarded particularly in Ladies Kennel Association organizations, Mrs. Spira proceeded to breed with skill and devotion, and in this endeavour she was greatly assisted by her husband, probably the best known veterinary surgeon and physician in Australia, Harold R. Spira, B. V. Sc., M. R. C. V. S. , H. D. A. Harry Spira is known not only for his brilliant veterinary skills but also as being one of the most talented of Australia's all-breed judges. Many clubs have him to thank for acting as their patron. He figured most prominently in the establishment of the Basset breed in Australia, is the Honorary Vet to the Royal Agricultural Society of New South Wales, and a member of their Consultative Council, has judged in every State of Australia and New Zealand, and is Chairman of the Judges Training Scheme in N. S. W. A member of the Kennel Club of England, he has been invited to judge at Cruft's. One of his great ambitions is to judge in the United States.

The Pindom Kennel, without doubt, is the leading one in Australia and most, if not all other breeders started with this stock. The original kennel inmates were Tasso Little Red Eva, sired by Brazen of Tavey out of Kanoon of Tavey; and Tasso Simba, fathered also by Brazen and mothered by Tasso Gypsy. For reasons of outcrossing, new imports had to be introduced by 1962, as by this time Mr. and Mrs. Spira had stimulated interest in the breed by often giving away a puppy as a gift to a fancier in another State. Human help was also needed, so the Spiras enlisted the assistance of Mr. and Mrs. Dennis Glackin, also of Sydney, and together in partnership the following dogs were imported: Rehpin King of Spades, Reary Ace High of Ardenoak, and Ardenoak Pineapply Doll. All of these dogs were blended in with the Pindom stock and produced a genetic lift and improvement in general "type."

The next import to follow in the early sixties was a blue and tan dog, Miss E. Pohl's Shumah Smokey Joe. But this dog was not used heavily in the foundation of the breed, probably because most breeders shied off colour problems. Around this time Mrs. Doris Mittler of Toowoomba, Queensland, also imported two British Min-Pins, Reary Hot Canary (which, although basically from English stock has some American dogs in its pedigree, including Vagabond's Deuce of Hearts) and Reary Christmas Fairy (of similar pedigree to the male but also featuring Stars Salute of Geddesburg and Sparkle of Geddesburg). One of her puppies, Minreh Auroral, was incorporated into the Pindom Kennel. The next link in the chain of history was forged by Mrs. M. Kneipp of Sydney in her purchase of initial Pindom bitches and the importation of a dog, Shumah Perry, and a bitch, Shumah Kiltie, from the United Kingdom. Prominent in these dogs' pedigrees is English Ch. Shumah Tio Pepe and Ch. Culandhu Para Handy. "Perry" and "Kiltie" in recent times have been purchased by Phillip and Elaine Cross of Sydney, whose Minelphi prefix is now well established. Particular mention amongst New South Wales breeders must also be given to Mr. and Mrs. T. Shannon, whose Shanlaw prefix, based on original Pindom stock, is greatly respected. Mr. and Mrs. L. Friend are other dedicated breeders who have set a high standard, not forgetting Rothwell Kennels, whose Pindom Lord Jordon and Lady Fran are frequent winners.

The story would not be complete without recognition of Mrs. Joan Hodges, who, besides having the distinction of exporting an Australian-bred Min-Pin to Hawaii, must be given a bouquet for her time consuming, but I imagine self-imposed, labour of love, in collating all American breed publications, stereotyping all this information and sending it to breed fanciers who have expressed an interest. Mrs. Hodges is the first in Australia to think seriously along the lines of importing an American Min-Pin directly from the States, and her idea was greatly encouraged by Dr. Buris R. Boshell of Birmingham, Alabama. Despite, however, the extremely generous offer of the gift of an American champion by Dr. Boshell, she found that the transportation expenses involved were beyond her means, and, with great reluctance, she had to cease negotiations along these lines.

Fortunate as was the breed with the Spiras of Turramurra, N. S. W., its luck extended South of the Border to Victoria. A lifelong friend of the Spiras was given Pindom Lady Davina, the much loved "Little Pip." This friend is Mr. Frank Longmore, acknowledged throughout Australia as one of our most distinguished and knowledgeable all-breed judges, and one always ready to help the novice, endeavoring to school the beginner along the right lines. His Rockwood Kennels, one time famous for its gun dogs, have produced some notable Min-Pins, including Rockwood Red Acre, a challenge winner at the Melbourne Royal, and Rockwood Princess Ann, the latter dog owned by Mrs. T. Henderson, whose show entries are firm evidence of breed support. Rumor has it that her puppy acquisition, Shawnlaw Sonny Boy, is destined for greatness.

And so we come to the present. The writer of this chapter has no claim to distinction in the past history of the breed. Bassets, Dalmatians, and Cocker Spaniels have been his former love. The Spira influence is, however, strong, and during a visit to his home on a judging appointment in Rockhampton, Harry Spira, with typical generosity, gave a Min-Pin to Mrs. L. B. Nicholson, the lady who so kindly looks after the house of this bachelor fancier. Thus "Tiny" Nicholson came to 134 George Street, a little black and tan bitch puppy in company with the late lamented "Tiger" Tucker purchased at the same time. These pups rejoiced in the titles of Pindom Lady Rocket and Pindom Lord Rebel. "Tiger's" lifespan was, however, very brief. He fell to the temptation of a dog murderer's bait thrown into his exercise yard. The spark of interest had been kindled, however, and hence across the world to England and America flew the correspondence whose final outcome is yet to be known but which has been responsible to date for the importation into Australia of the elegant and beautiful bitch, now an Australian champion with one Best-in-Show and two Reserve Best-in-Show wins, Birling Starlight. Joining her is Birling Mr. Jinks, son of English Ch. Birling Painted Lady, the all time top bitch in England. Starlight's sire is England's answer to the world-famous Rebel-Roc's Casanova von Kurt—English Ch. Birling Wawocan Constellation, Reserve Toy in 1967 at Cruft's and the holder in retirement of 26 English C. C.'s. Both Starlight and Jinks are from the kennel of Lionel Hamilton Renwick of Upend, New Market, England, whose knowledge of the breed in the United Kingdom is unrivaled.

American imports Bo-Mar's Ambassador and Bo-Mar's Jenny Lou arrived recently and will be blended with the Birling lines.

154

The Miniature Pinscher
In South Africa

The Miniature Pinscher was first introduced into South Africa by a Mr. de la Chanaie, who was connected with the French Embassy in South Africa some twenty years ago. However, the breed was little known in South Africa until the late '50s when stock imported from England by breeders in the Cape Town and Johannesburg areas brought the breed to the attention of dog fanciers.

Today there are many imported Min-Pins in the country. Those brought in as breeding stock for the Cape Town and Johannesburg kennels came from the kennels of Lionel Hamilton Renwick of Suffolk, England, although one dog, Burman Chamna Gunga Din, was imported from the kennel of Mrs. M. Sharp of the British Isles.

It is interesting to note that despite the fact that Mr. de la Chanaie's activities were little publicized, offspring of his stock, titled "de la Chanaie," appear in the pedigree of virtually every Min-Pin whelped in South Africa today. It is also interesting to note that the name of Ch. Bel-Roc's Dobe von Enztal from the United States appears in a number of the Min-Pin pedigrees.

The breed Standard in South Africa calls for height at shoulder to be from ten to twelve inches. Although both black and rust as well as red occur, the reds apparently are somewhat more popular. Cropping of ears is prohibited in South Africa, so there is an effort to breed dogs with naturally erect ears.

Among South Africa's enthusiastic breeders are Mr. and Mrs. Henry Stephens of Carletonville, a gold mining town about fifty miles from Johannesburg. Half-Tot, their ten inch Miniature Pinscher bitch, is the dam of the five puppies whelped in a single litter and pictured on page 10 of this book. Three days after Half-Tot's litter was whelped, her dam, Lenhenri's Nancy, whelped a litter of eight puppies, which appears to be a record number for the breed in South Africa. Unfortunately, one of the eight died soon after birth. However, the remaining seven have continued to thrive and they and their dam are also pictured on page 10.

Int., Swedish, Danish, and Norwegian Ch. "Saroya," owned by A. Rätz.

Ch. Birling Blissful, Top Min-Pin for 1962.

The Miniature Pinscher
In Other Countries

It was in Germany, the native country of the Min-Pin, in the year 1863, that the first official dog show was held where dogs were judged on the basis of their physical appearance and their presumed ability to perform whatever task had been specified as appropriate for their breed. The report of that first German dog show states that the little dogs exhibited there were the main interest of the visiting ladies. Unfortunately, the "little dogs" are not identified by breed, so it is impossible to say whether any Min-Pins were among those shown. Twenty years later, however, the Min-Pin was found among the breeds registered by the German Kennel Club (*Verein Zur Veredelung der Hunderacen für Deutschland*). And a judges' report of a dog show at Hannover that same year states that several German Min-Pins, "of the smallest bred," were entered.

Although the breed had been recognized officially in 1880 and the official breed Standard included in the German studbook, it was not until September 16, 1900, that the first Miniature Pinscher Specialty Show in Germany took place. The show was held at Stuttgart and ninety-three dogs were entered.

From 1900 to 1914 the breed flourished in Germany, and interest was high. Among the famous Min-Pin kennels producing outstanding stock through the years was the v. Gretelheim Kennel, which was established prior to World War I and which bred the 1937 World Ch. Olga v. Gretelheim—as well as many other outstanding dogs. Other famous kennels that consistently bred fine Min-Pins through the years include v. Alztal, v. Biefang, v. Geisenfeld, v. Jagerheim, v. Kaltenhausen, v. Kamphausen, v. Leerort, v. Nussgarten, v. Otterberg, v. Sachsenhausen, v. Siegerland, v. Sterntor, and v. d. Thumblinger Hohe. When pedigrees are traced back far enough, many of the foregoing kennel names will be found among the ancestors of current American Min-Pin winners.

German Min-Pins are usually red, or black and tan—rarely blue or chocolate. The same is true in Belgium, where the breed has followed much the same path of development as in other West

European Countries. According to G. Stoesser, Secretary and Treasurer of the *Club Belge du Schnauzer et Pinscher,* current Min-Pin kennels include Kennel "Petits Trésors," owned by Madame Gillissen at Liége; Kennel "Van Lentegeluk," owned by Madame Pots at Brussels; Kennel "du Castel Sébastian," owned by Monsieur Decleyn at Morlanwelz; Kennel "Van Westkamp," owned by Monsieur Misselyn at Kuurne; and Kennel "de la sources des Mottes," owned by Madame Cloquette at Froyennes.

The history of Miniature Pinschers in Denmark begins in 1905, when six dogs of the breed were benched at a dog show—four males and two females. Through the years, the number of Min-Pins benched at the shows has gradually increased, but for the past quarter century the bloodlines of the Ajas Kennel have predominated both among the Danish show winners and among the Danish dogs exported to other countries.

The Ajas Kennel was founded in 1920 by Mr. K. Johansen, who authored the first book on the breed. He utilized the Herzhof, von der Lichtweishöhle, von Helluland-Dallacker, and von Gretelheim lines from Germany, interbreeding with a few bloodlines from Norway, Sweden and the Netherlands. Ajas Min-Pins have continued to rank as the best in Europe. Most of the dogs from this line are black and tan, but some reds are also produced, as well as a few chocolates.

The Miniature Pinscher Club of Holland came into being in1919, and among current breeders are some who started their kennels some fifty years ago—at the time the club was founded. Though kennels there are not so numerous as in some other European countries, some outstanding Min-Pins have been produced in Holland—particularly from the Kennel Trouwe Vriendjes, which has exported a number of fine dogs to other countries, as well as supplying breeding stock for other fanciers in Holland.

M. Priems v. d. Laak, of the Kennel "Petit Bonheur," has been active in breeding activities in Holland and recently imported dogs from England and Sweden for use in her breeding program.

The Japanese Miniature Pinscher Club was organized only recently, and the first all Min-Pin Show in Japan was held on the roof of the Shirokiya Department Store on October 15, 1967. Eighty-two dogs were entered in the show, which was judged by Mr. S. T. Culliton. Best in Show was won by Ch. Shelger of House

158

Enocki, a black and rust male owned by Mr. Y. Enocki.

The popularity of the Miniature Pinscher is increasing in Japan and a number of dogs have been imported from Germany as well as from the United States. Among the imports are dogs from Bailes, Bo-Mar, and Jay-Mac Kennels, including Ch. Surprise in Black, Ch. Sandyhill Comanchero of Bo-Mar, Ch. Bo-Mar's Dark Delia, and Ch. Bo-Mar's Drum Son of Jay-Mac.

Miss Mickey Carmichael sculpting model for the Sir Ius of the Hill Trophy.

His Day

An Ode to Ch. Bo-Mar's Drummer Boy

By Barbara Andrews

He walked into the ring today,
His satin coat aglow.
He faced the Judge and seemed to say,
"I am here to win, you know."

"Behold my beauty unsurpassed,
A princely guy, I am.
I'm royally bred throughout my past,
Find better if you can."

An egotist this boy of mine?
I'm sure the Judge agreed.
But when he searched his heart and mind,
He gave him Best-of-Breed.

He won the Group, with flash and fire
And never missed his stride.
He strutted like a country squire
Beside himself with pride.

Now here he comes, his head held high
Stepping light and proud.
True and black, his eager eyes
Survey the waiting crowd.

He plants his feet and firmly stands.
Somehow, he seems to know,
The Trophy in the Judge's hands,
Proclaims him BEST-IN-SHOW.